# PRACT
# SOCIAL

### Series Editor: Jo Campling

### BASW

Social work is at an important stage in its development. All professions must be responsive to changing social and economic conditions if they are to meet the needs of those they serve. This series focuses on sound practice and the specific contribution which social workers can make to the well-being of our society in the 1990s.

The British Association of Social Workers has always been conscious of its role in setting guidelines for practice and in seeking to raise professional standards. The conception of the Practical Social Work series arose from a survey of BASW members to discover where they, the practitioners in social work, felt there was the most need for new literature. The response was overwhelming and enthusiastic, and the result is a carefully planned, coherent series of books. The emphasis is firmly on practice, set in a theoretical framework. The books will inform, stimulate and promote discussion, thus adding to the further development of skills and high professional standards. All the authors are practitioners and teachers of social work, representing a wide variety of experience.

### JO CAMPLING

Robert Adams *Self-Help, Social Work and Empowerment*

David Anderson *Social Work and Mental Handicap*

Robert Brown, Stanley Bute and Peter Ford *Social Workers at Risk*

Alan Butler and Colin Pritchard *Social Work and Mental Illness*

Roger Clough *Residential Work*

David M. Cooper and David Ball *Social Work and Child Abuse*

Veronica Coulshed *Management in Social Work*

Veronica Couldshed *Social Work Practice: An introduction (2nd edn)*

Paul Daniel and John Wheeler *Social Work and Local Politics*

Peter R. Day *Sociology in Social Work Practice*

Lena Dominelli *Anti-Racist Social Work:A Challenge for White Practitioners and Educators*

Celia Doyle *Working with Abused Children*

Geoff Fimister *Welfare Rights Work in Social Services*

Kathy Ford and Alan Jones *Student Supervision*

Alison Froggatt *Family Work with Elderly People*

Danya Glaser and Stephen Frost *Child Sexual Abuse*

Gill Gorell Barnes *Working with Families*

Jalna Hanmer and Daphne Statham *Women and Social Work:Towards a Woman-Centred Practice*

Tony Jeffs and Mark Smith *Youth Work*

Michael Kerfoot and Alan Butler *Problems of Childhood and Adolescence*

Mary Marshall *Social Work with Old People (2nd edn)*

Paula Nicolson and Rowan Bayne *Applied Psychology for Social Workers (2nd edn)*

Kieran O'Hagan *Crisis Intervention in Social Services*

Michael Oliver *Social Work with Disabled People*

Lisa Parkinson *Separation, Divorce and Families*

Malcolm Payne *Social Care in the Community*

Malcolm Payne *Working in Teams*

John Pitts*Working with Young Offenders*

Michael Preston-Shoot *Effective Groupwork*

Carole R. Smith *Adoption and Fostering: Why and How*

Carole R. Smith *Social Work with the Dying and Bereaved*

Carole R. Smith, Marty T. Lane and Terry Walshe *Child Care and the Courts*

Alan Twelvetrees *Community Work (2nd edn)*

Hilary Walker and Bill Beaumount (eds) *Working with Offenders*

FORTHCOMING TITLES

Jim Barber *Social Work Practice*

Lynne Berry, Crescy Cannan and Karen Lyons *Social Work in Europe*

Suzy Braye and Michael Preston-Shoot *Practising Social Work Law*

Suzy Croft and Peter Beresford *Involving the Consumer*

Angela Everitt, Pauline Hardiker, Jane Littlewood and Audrey Millender *Applied Research for Better Practice*

Michael Freeman *The Children's Act 1989*

Cordelia Grimwood and Ruth Poppleston *Women, Management and Care*

David Hebblewhite and Tom Leckie *Social Work with Addictions*

Paul Henderson and David Francis *Working with Rural Communities*

Rosemary Jefferson and Mike Shooter *Preparing for Practice*

Jeremy Kearney and Dave Evans *A Systems Approach to Social Work*

Joyce Lishman *Communication and Social Work*

Carole Lupton (ed) *Working with Violence*

Graham McBeath and Stephen Webb *The Politics of Social Work*

Steven Shardlow and Mark Doel *Practice: Learning and Teaching*

Gill Stewart and John Stewart *Social Work and Housing*

# Beyond Casework

James G. Barber

**M**
MACMILLAN

First published 1991 by
THE MACMILLAN PRESS LTD
Houndmills, Basingstoke, Hampshire RG21 2XS
and London
Companies and representatives
throughout the world

ISBN 0–333–54875–2 hardcover
ISBN 0–333–54876–0 paperback

A catalogue record for this book is available
from the British Library

Printed in Hong Kong

Reprinted 1993

**Series Standing Order**

If you would like to receive future titles in this series as they are
published, you can make use of our standing order facility. To
place a standing order please contact your bookseller or, in case
of difficulty, write to us at the address below with your name and
address and the name of the series. Please state with which title
you wish to begin your standing order. (If you live outside the
UK we may not have the rights for your area, in which case we
will forward your order to the publisher concerned.)

Standing Order Service, Macmillan Distribution Ltd,
Houndmills, Basingstoke, Hampshire, RG21 2XS, England

# Contents

# List of Figures

To my parents, Carmel and Jim, with love and gratitude

# 1

# Towards a Politically Progressive Model of Casework Practice

Because of its apparent indifference to broader political realities, casework has always been a favourite target for the more radical critics of social work practice. This radical critique of casework can be traced back at least as far as C. Wright Mills, who protested that: 'Present institutions train several kinds of persons – such as judges and social workers – to think in terms of "situations". Their activities and mental outlook are set within the existing norms of society: in their professional work they tend to have an occupationally trained incapacity to rise above "cases"' (Mills, 1943, p. 171). Mills points out that the tendency to identify social work with casework inevitably results in psychologistic practice models which seek solutions to human suffering in psychopathology and interpersonal relationships. Such models, he claims, are nothing but subterfuge; they are a confidence trick designed to provide non-political solutions to politically-inflicted misery. Over the years radical social theorists have kept up their attack on what they see as a retreat by social work into casework (for example, Galper, 1975; Bailey and Brake, 1977; Simpkin, 1983). Society, they claim, is built on conflict of interests, and the failure of social workers to address the underlying political causes of individual distress implicates the entire profession in the domination of the poor by the economically powerful.

1

In his classic book, *Blaming the Victim*, William Ryan (1971) provides a detailed discussion of the consequences of reductionism. Ryan wrote his book after working for some years as a psychologist in the so-called American 'War of Poverty' during the presidency of Lyndon B. Johnson. Ryan came to believe that this expensive and well-intentioned plan was fundamentally flawed. The basic aim of the programme was to identify how the poor could be trained to compete more successfully for their share of the national wealth. In Ryan's view the problem with this idea is that it assumes the poor are poor because *they* are deficient in some way, not because social structures exclude them. To the extent that human service workers seek to 'help' the poor by changing them in some way, these workers are 'blaming the victims' for problems which are not of their making. Similarly, Caplan and Nelson (1973) have referred to the process of focusing on individuals to the exclusion of social and contextual factors as a 'person-blame attributional bias'. This biased perception of reality is evident in the tendency to attribute causal significance to person-centred variables which may be found in association with the social problem in question. Like Ryan, Caplan and Nelson maintain that this person-blame bias serves the latent and ultimately cynical social function of freeing the government and other primary cultural institutions from blame for social problems. The implication of this trenchant, if by now familiar, critique of social casework is that 'legitimate' practice involves radical, perhaps even revolutionary, social change. No doubt readers will differ as to the need for radical reform but Ryan's (1971) and Caplan and Nelson's (1973) call to eschew exclusively reductionist solutions can be affirmed no matter what one's political convictions. Reductionism misses the point of human problems by failing to recognise the intrinsic social dimension of the human condition.

This book accepts the radical objection to an over-reliance on psychological solutions but it repudiates the doctrinaire approach to social change that commonly follows. Thus it objects not to radical social analysis, but to the unrealistic and discouraging claim that casework practice is antithetical to social change. Indeed, the book seeks to develop a workable approach to social change which is *based* on casework. It assumes that in a profession which is itself relatively powerless, political influence can be exercised best by mobilising individual 'cases'. Even more importantly, the book assumes that marginalised individuals themselves have a right and a responsibility to work for change. The result is an approach to practice which conceives of social work as a process that moves from casework to community organisation as the intervention plan gathers momentum.

The need for such approaches to practice has become particularly pressing in the United Kingdom since the adoption by the Tory government in 1989–90 of the so-called Griffiths' Report (1988). The primary objective of this report is to support disabled people in the community wherever possible rather than consigning them to institutions. To achieve this, local authorities have been charged with responsibility for coordinating alternative care arrangements outside institutions and for ensuring that the elderly, mentally ill and intellectually disabled in the community are the subject of individual case plans and adequate support services. In their likely role as case managers under the new regime, social workers will be thrust even more forcefully into the community, where they will need to be skilled in advocacy and lobbying to ensure that their clients' right to an adequate level of support is protected. Moreover, clients will need to be both vocal and organised if their dispersion within the community is not to alienate and disenfranchise them even further.

**The social work perspective**

It is most ironic that social workers should have attracted so much criticism for their failure to make the connection between personal troubles and political issues because social work is supposedly *dedicated* to the broader social factors involved in client problems. Indeed, a focus on environmental factors is probably the single most obvious thread running through the history of social work literature. As Werner Boehm (1958) put it more than 30 years ago:

Social work seeks to enhance the social functioning of individuals, singularly and in groups, by activities focused on their social relationships which constitute interaction between individuals and their environments. These activities can be grouped into three functions: restoration of impaired capacity, provision of individual and social resources, and prevention of social dysfunction. (p. 18)

This environmental perspective has been restated in various ways by various authors over the years. Ten years later, for example, William Gordon (1969) asserted:

We conclude, therefore, that the central target of technical social work practice is *matching* something in person and situation – that is, intervening by whatever methods and means necessary to help people be in situations where their capabilities are sufficiently matched with the demands of the situation to 'make a go of it'. (p. 6)

Perhaps the most significant statement of the social work role in the last twenty years was made by Harriet Bartlett (1970) for the American National Association of Social Workers (NASW). In her book on the topic, Bartlett speaks of the social work concern with social functioning, by which she means the relationship between people and the demands made on them by the environment. For Bartlett, social work involves a 'dual focus' on person and situation. In her own words: 'attention is now directed primarily to what goes on between people and environment through the exchange between them. This dual focus ties them together. Thus person and situation, people and environment, are encompassed in a single concept, which requires that they be constantly reviewed together' (p. 116). The NASW statement on social work continues to provide the inspiration for social work education throughout the Western world. Social workers lay claim to a generic body of knowledge and skills which can be brought to bear in a wide range of situations. The foundation for generic social work is this perspective on the human condition; it is a view which supposedly is carried into every context in which social work is practised.

Many social work authors have come to embrace general systems theory as a way of operationalising the social work commitment to this holistic perspective on human problems (for example Janchill, 1969; Hartman, 1970; Strean, 1971; Goldstein, 1973; Pincus and Minahan, 1973; Stein, 1974; Vickery, 1974; Compton and Galaway, 1984). The work of these authors is often replete with jargon but the basic idea is really quite simple. The general systems view of society is an analogy; it is a way of thinking about the world which draws a parallel between the way society operates and the way biological systems operate. Just as the study of biology has shown us that all living things, be they individual creatures or entire ecosystems, are a complex organisation of parts working together to survive, general systems theory conceives of the entire social world and all the regions, communities, even families and other domestic units that make up the world as interdependent parts of a much greater whole. All these parts (or sub-systems) provide the conditions for the survival of the other parts. It is this *inter*dependence or *inter*action between the parts that is the basic insight of general systems theory. Since change in any part of the system affects the system as a whole, systems can only be understood when the transactions occurring within and between sub-systems are understood. The systems view ensures that people are not thought of as isolated individuals but as elements in a social system which includes but also transcends them. As Compton and Galaway (1984) have put it: 'The systems model shifts attention from characteristics possessed by individual units to interaction and relatedness' (p. 113).

One of the simplest and clearest expositions of the systems theory perspective was provided by the social developmental psychologist Ury Bronfenbrenner (1979), who wrote of the need to understand the 'ecological environment' inhabited by the individual under investigation. Bronfenbrenner conceived of the ecological environment topologically as a set of nested structures extending far beyond the immediate situation directly experienced by the person. Equally important are connections between other persons present in the setting and their indirect influence on the person through their effect on those who deal with him or her first-hand. To capture this interdependence of the various possible levels of analysis, Bronfenbrenner employed a diagrammatic representation of concentric structures, each contained within the next as shown in Figure 1.1.

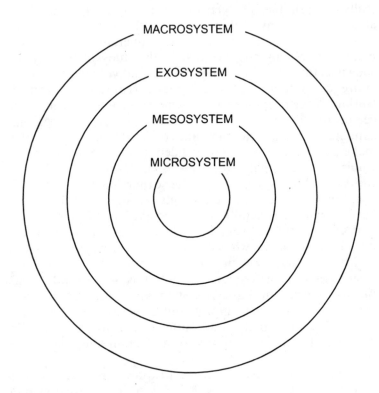

**Figure 1.1** *The ecological environment*

At the lowest level of analysis – and one which is taken for granted in Bronfenbrenner's model – is the individual client. Clearly, all casework must begin with a thorough assessment of the client and his or her view of the situation. Beyond that is the microsystem, or the pattern of activities, roles and interpersonal relations experienced by the client in a given setting. In other words, the microsystem is the client's immediate phenomenological environment. It contains all individuals and settings with which the client has a direct relationship, such as family members, the workplace, friendship networks, and so on. In order to understand the client's problem, then, we need to understand the interconnections between the client and others within his or her immediate setting. Beyond the microsystem is the mesosystem, or the interrelations among two or more settings in which the client actively participates. At this level of analysis, the social worker assesses relationships between the set of microsystems that comprise the client's life, such as the relationship between home and the workplace, or home and friendship networks. At a level beyond mesosystem analysis is the exosystem, which refers to one or more settings that do not involve the client as an active participant, but within which events occur that affect what happens in settings that do contain the client. Exosystem analysis in social work typically involves the assessment of social policy issues impinging on the client's problem. For example, the current policy of deinstitutionalisation in health and welfare services has many implications for social work clients and their microsystems. It often means, for example, that disabled clients are more reliant on their families and friends nowadays as institutions divest themselves of responsibility for the long-term care of disabled persons. Moreover, social work clients and their families may never even have heard the term deinstitutionalisation, let alone met any of the policy-makers responsible for its inception, yet an understanding of the policy may be essential in order to grasp all the dimensions of the disabled client's problem. The final level in Bronfenbrenner's model is the macrosystem, or consistencies in the form or content of lower-order systems (micro-, meso- and exo-) that exist at the level of the subculture or culture. An example of a macrosystem issue relevant to a child protection case would be Belsky's (1980) point that child abuse will persist so long as society continues to look upon children as the property of their parents rather than as separate individuals with inalienable rights of their own.

Though usually stated differently from Bronfenbrenner, various social work authors have incorporated ecological concepts into their practice models: for example, Germain and Gitterman's (1980) so-called 'life model' represents one popular attempt within social work to articulate an ecological approach to problem assessment. According to Germain and Gitterman, the ecological perspective emphasises the life processes of adaptation and reciprocal interaction between people and their social and physical environments. Accordingly, Germain and Gitterman assert that problems in living must be confronted at more than one level. Specifically, human problems are said to arise in three interrelated areas of living: (a) life transitions, (b) environmental pressures, and (c) interpersonal processes. Life transitions include changes that occur developmentally (such as the adaptations required during parenthood), as well as changes resulting from crisis (for example, the loss of a partner). Consistent with their formulation, Germain and Gitterman direct the worker to assess the client's problem at three levels simultaneously: first, the worker needs to determine the life transitional problems and needs of the client; second, the client's interpersonal relationships need to be assessed to determine whether any maladaptive interpersonal processes are in evidence; and third, environmental problems and needs must be identified. The aim of this multiple-level problem analysis is to find ways of increasing the client's adaptive capacities *at the same time* as increasing the responsiveness of the environment to the client. Once again, therefore, social work's commitment to the broad or systemic view of human problems comes through.

Both for reasons of expediency and professional status social workers are frequently guilty of psychological reductionism despite the systemic models from which they operate. Psychotherapy and family therapy are exalted activities among many caseworkers in the Western world, perhaps because this kind of work makes the lowly social worker appear more like a psychiatrist or clinical psychologist. Moreover, individual clients and their families are easier to influence than the higher level systems identified by Bronfenbrenner. Indeed, intervention plans that look beyond individuals and their families to broader systemic influences are frequently censured by the organisations that employ social workers. In a perverse twist to this drift towards psychological reductionism, social work therapists often retain the language of systems theory while limiting the unit of analysis to the most immediate social unit, the microsystem. Less direct, but potentially more significant, systemic influences are simply ignored. However, for those who genuinely seek to do social casework, there can be no escaping a broader social assessment. It is the starting point for social work intervention and arguably the single most important component of the case plan.

## The practice model

It is clearly insufficient for the caseworker to have a well-developed understanding of a problem if he or she has no strategy for action, so the framework outlined in Figure 1.2 seeks to integrate the dual tasks of assessment and intervention into one practice model.

Under the present model, Bronfenbrenner's ecological approach to assessment has been adapted to take account of the fact that social work assessment is rarely, if ever, a once-and-for-all activity. Far from being completed before intervention begins, the process of trying to solve the problem usually casts light on the problem itself. Accordingly, the first phase of our practice model (the casework phase) emphasises the more immediate and obvious system levels of the individual, the microsystem and the mesosystem. This does not seek to relieve the worker of responsibility for taking the broadest view possible from the outset; instead, it recognises that in the early stages of casework lower-level factors will normally be the most salient. Indeed, because it can take considerable practice experience to become fully aware of the broader or more complex systemic issues helping to sustain a client's problem, it is not uncommon for caseworkers to remain at the lower system levels until they have handled a number of similar cases. For example, while the pattern of pathological relationships within a

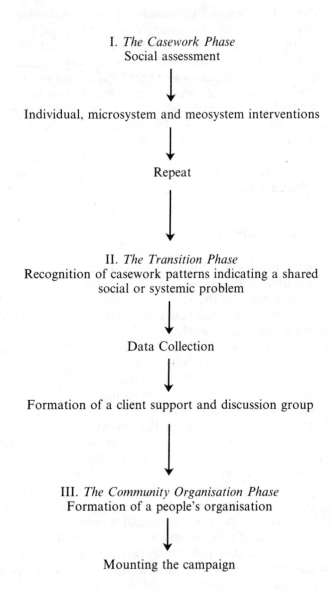

I. *The Casework Phase*
Social assessment

Individual, microsystem and meosystem interventions

Repeat

II. *The Transition Phase*
Recognition of casework patterns indicating a shared
social or systemic problem

Data Collection

Formation of a client support and discussion group

III. *The Community Organisation Phase*
Formation of a people's organisation

Mounting the campaign

**Figure 1.2.**   *A model of social work practice*

psychiatric patient's family (a microsystem problem) may be manifestly apparent early on in the life of a case, it can take the accumulated experience of many cases to appreciate fully the involvement of inadequate after-care facilities, or discriminatory admission policies within community-based programmes (mesosystem factors); nevertheless, all these factors may play a role in a client's apparent inability to survive outside a psychiatric hospital. Thus, our practice model further proposes that Phase I tends to be repeated for some time before the caseworker moves on to higher system level activity. However, this latter proposition is clearly not essential to the model. For some workers the transition from individual problems to broader systemic issues will occur quite easily and spontaneously while others will take longer, often depending on the complexity of the issues involved.

It should also be stressed that even if Phase I activity does represent an *inadequate* response to the casework problem, this does not mean that the intervention is of no benefit. And from the worker's viewpoint, the contacts made and insights gained in doing the work will provide a basis for the people's organisation that should be the culmination of the caseworker's intervention. Both because clients normally derive short-term benefits from Phase I activity and because this work lays the foundation for higher-level activity, the present model rejects as being simplistic the inference that 'legitimate' social work has a system-change focus in contrast to the 'illegitimate' client-change focus of casework.

Perhaps the single most crucial point in our practice model actually occurs inside the caseworker's head. It is the point when the worker begins to see patterns or regularities in the problems confronted by his or her clients and recognises the need for change at broader system levels as well. We can refer to this as the transition phase for it is at this point that the worker truly shifts the focus of practice from individual problems to social and political issues. The transition phase would begin, for example, when a worker recognises the many social problems that the parents of neglected children have in common. Many of the child protection worker's clients are likely to be poor, unemployed, socially isolated and young. In other words, they are excluded from the mainstream of society and the worker recognises that until child protection problems are addressed at this level casework will be of limited value. As well as this basic insight, Phase II involves the worker making decisions about what he or she can do to address the higher system level issues.

Ultimately, however, the mandate for this higher level activity must come from our clients. Moreover, the success of the worker's efforts is likely to depend on the involvement of clients. The voice of an individual social worker calling for some new service or the alteration of existing social policy is unlikely to evoke much response from policy-makers. But when that voice is joined with those of a well-organised client group the call invariably becomes more pressing. Thus, Phase II in casework involves the social worker in collecting evidence of the need for change and in making contact with the individuals who will form the core of a people's organisation. As we will see in Chapter 6, there are a number of possible approaches to compiling evidence but it should be stressed at this point that the process is not primarily a scientific one, it is a tactical move designed to attract public sympathy and attention to the need for reform. For this reason, anecdotal evidence extracted from the caseworker's own casenotes can often be a more powerful means of establishing need than more scientifically accurate methods, such as the use of area surveys and social indicators.

While gathering this evidence, the worker must also start bringing clients and others affected by the problem together to gain mutual support and share their perceptions of the problem. For example, the parents of psychiatric patients struggling to maintain their children at home, or single mothers trying to deal with poverty and the demands of 24 hour child-care can derive great comfort from the support of others in a similar predicament. Perhaps more importantly, these informal groups almost invariably come to reflect on ways of improving their lot through communal action. During Phase III, then, the task of the social worker is to promote this group support and reflection, as well as to share the evidence he or she has been gathering in support of the need for change. The information will help guide group reflection and convince members of the need for action.

In his book, *Don't Mourn For Me . . . Organise*, David Scott (1981) argues that non-government welfare organisations have a central role to play in the planning and provision of social services, but that they will continue to be relegated to remedial social work activity until they 'organise' and make demands on the government bureaucracies charged with responsibility for public welfare. Scott sees a role for voluntary organisations as a mediating structure between the client and the state, (for instance, as a vehicle for collectivising individual concerns and thereby empowering clients in their dealings with public policy-makers). Assuming clients themselves are closely involved in this process, the voluntary organisation has a further benefit: it educates the poor and marginalised in the skills necessary to bring about social change. These, then, are the aims of the third phase of casework practice. During this phase the worker seeks to build a client organisation around an issue of vital importance to clients themselves and to engage them in the struggle for change.

The transition from client to social activist is not an easy one to make as it normally involves a profound shift in the client's view of the world. Indeed, the remainder of this book is concerned with effecting this kind of change in clients. Having looked in this chapter at the fundamental importance of the holistic perspective, we will look at the application of social casework theory to our practice model before considering tactics for the empowerment of individuals. It is argued that most social work clients are unaccustomed to controlling their lives and therfore are likely to be resigned to their lot. Accordingly, the assumption that nothing can change is one of the first probelms to be dealt with in casework and it requires interventions at the lower system levels of individual, microsystem and mesosytem. Chapter 4 takes up the particular complexities surrounding casework with involuntary clients. The very notion of involuntarism seems to contradict client empowerment, yet the reality is that many social work clients submit to intervention only under threat of legal retaliation. We will face up to this issue in Chapter 4 and explore a possible solution based on conflict-management strategies. Chapter 5 provides an overview of community work theory as a backdrop for our own approach to community organising. Chapter 6 moves to mediating work and looks at the formation of informal client groups and outlines methods for collecting evidence of the need for broader systemic change. Chapter 7 outlines the practical tasks involved in building a people's organisation and mounting a campaign of social action. In the final chapter we will return to the radical critique of social work and consider the extent to which our model is likely to satisfy the objections reviewed in this chapter.

# 2

# Casework Theory

The following brief history of social casework theory is intended to introduce some of the more influential ideas that have informed social work practice over the years. More than this, it seeks to clarify the reasons why social work should have attracted so much criticism from radical writers and to identify the problems in previous theorising that our model seeks to address. The list of theoretical approaches is not exhaustive, nor is it strictly chronological. No discipline proceeds in an orderly fashion from one paradigm to the next. Indeed, it could be argued that the divisions between approaches are somewhat artificial; as we shall see, the social work literature displays a penchant for incorporating ideas from multiple sources, making it difficult to assign some authors to one camp or the other. The review has been divided into 'pre-generalist' and 'generalist' eras because it is fair to say that a discontinuous shift in theorising occurred in the 1970s when caseworkers began searching for common ground with their social work colleagues from other fields. However, even a cursory glance at the dates of the publications cited will demonstrate that pre-generalist approaches continue to attract adherents today.

## The Pre-Generalist Era

*Psychosocial Theory*

The intellectual origins of social casework are normally traced back to the publication in 1917 of Mary E. Richmond's *Social Diagnosis*. Richmond's two central themes were: (a) that clients and their problems have to be

15

*individualised,* and (b) that successful casework requires careful *diagnosis.* Her view was that a clear understanding of what needed to be done would emerge from a systematic study of all the 'facts' of the case: if the caseworker amassed enough 'facts', the intervention plan would follow logically. Richmond called her method of collecting and evaluating facts 'social study and social diagnosis', but she had little interest in social change. Indeed, one of her central assumptions was that casework could only be conducted on a case-by-case basis. As Richmond (1922) herself put it, social casework is about 'those processes which develop personality through adjustments consciously effected, individual by individual, between men [sic] and their social environment' (p. 98). Richmond initiated what became known as the 'diagnostic school' of social work and such was the influence of her ideas that casework (though not necessarily her own approach to it) became the dominant social work method for the next half century (cf. Germain and Hartman, 1980). Richmond's work was taken up and elaborated by a succession of theorists including Hamilton (1937, 1941, 1951), Austin (1948) and F. Hollis (1964, 1968, 1977), all of whom incorporated ideas drawn from other sources, especially Freudian psychology and general systems theory. In recognition of its changing emphases the diagnostic school became 'psychosocial casework' and although the approach retains its emphasis on individualised diagnosis and treatment (Turner, 1983), its language and units of analysis are now more closely aligned to the person-in-situation perspective that has become the trademark of social work practice.

Under psychosocial theory (cf. F. Hollis, 1970; Turner, 1987) the initial phase of treatment is vital, for it is then that a thorough (not to say laborious) assessment is made of all the overt and covert reasons for contact, and a therapeutic relationship with the client is established. The broad prescriptions for practice during this phase are distinctly clinical and directed somewhat pre-emptively at 'engaging the client in *treatment*' (F. Hollis, 1970, p. 43). Following the early work of Richmond, psychosocial casework does promote indirect or environmental interventions as well as direct clinical work, but even today it retains a very narrow understanding of what constitutes 'the environment', resulting in social interventions which usually seek little more than to mobilise or modify existing community resources. Consequently, despite an expressed commitment to psychosocial interventions, psychosocial casework has been roundly criticised for its refusal to address the structural origins of casework problems and for taking refuge in psychotherapy and remedial welfare services (Mayer and Timms, 1970; Meyer, 1987).

## The functional approach

Whereas disciples of the diagnostic school began turning to Freudian psychology to provide the coherent theory of personality that was lacking in Richmond's (1917, 1922) early work, a new school based on the writings of Otto Rank also emerged at around the same time as a new and antagonistic alternative (Robinson, 1930; Taft, 1937). The so-called 'functional school' of social casework objected to what it considered to be a mechanistic view of human nature inherent in Freudian psychology, and in particular to Freud's over-emphasis on psychopathology. For its part, the functional school held a more positive view of humankind as rational creators of their own lives, motivated by higher needs such as those for health and self-fulfilment. Indeed, there is an existential flavour to functional casework. Unlike the Freudian view of emotion and behaviour as emanating from the dark struggle between unconscious desires and the internalised restrictions of harsh external reality, the functional school thought of clients as people engaged in a hopeful, even noble, act of self-creation and as capable of modifying themselves and their environments according to their own rational purposes.

The different emphases found expression in casework terms like 'helping' and 'enabling' (Smalley, 1967) rather than 'diagnosis' and 'treatment', but perhaps the school's most important idea, and the one from which it derived its name, is the notion of agency *function* as the foundation of client-worker relationships (Taft, 1937). The functional caseworker's primary task is to administer the agency's programme (for example, child protection or income security), not to 'treat' clients; the client's capacity for positive self-direction is said to develop as a consequence of his or her use of the service. Thus, functional casework is strong on process issues, with the relationship between worker and client, and the experience of the service itself being seen as sufficient for psychological change to occur. As Smalley (1977) put it:

> Use of agency function has psychological as well as social value as an integral part of casework skill. What the agency can do and the conditions under which it can be done provide something for the client to come to grips with, so that he [sic] can find a way to use it positively and constructively in his own interest as this interest coincides with that of society. The client is helped to do this through the caseworker's relationship skill, which is directed toward assisting the client find his own purpose in relation to agency purpose and to experience perhaps more know-ingly, but at any rate more deeply than has been possible for him heretofore, a way of relating to others and of working to achieve purpose with the opportunity to modify that way constructively through experience in the social work relationship. (p. 1200)

Despite the functional school's view of itself as being more liberal than psychosocial casework, functional casework is at least as politically conservative, if not more so, than psychosocial casework. Not only is the primary objective psychological growth/change within the client, but the primacy of agency function has the effect of cementing caseworkers to the status quo. According to the functional school, social work is indicated when society identifies a need that a number of people are unable to meet by their own efforts and, if not eventually met, will constitute a threat to society and to the welfare of the individuals experiencing that need. This is a remedial view of welfare and there is an obvious moral component to the functional school's defence of this view. For example, later in the same article Smalley declared that: 'the functional position is that as long as the caseworker is an employee of the agency, he [sic] is obliged to represent that agency and discharge its purpose in relation to those he serves' (p. 1204).

*The problem-solving approach*

Helen Harris Perlman (1957) tried to effect a truce in the long-running dispute between the psychosocial and diagnostic schools by drawing together some of the key ideas of both approaches in her influential textbook on casework practice. Perlman's basic assumption was that human living is a continuous problem-solving process and therefore that the goal of casework is not 'cure' but facilitation of an individual's capacity to cope with current problems. It is an approach which reduces the emphasis on psychopathology and the psychological legacy of childhood in favour of a more rational perspective focused on the present. A person's inability to deal with a problem is said to be due to some lack of *motivation, capacity* or *opportunity* to solve the problem. Casework therefore aims to tackle one or more of these impediments to problem resolution: to release and direct the client's motivation; to release and exercise the client's problem-solving capacities (sometimes referred to as ego functions); and/or to mobilise the resources and opportunities necessary to address the problem. As far as possible the problem is partialised and confined to that aspect of the situation which the client finds most distressing. Through resolving the current crisis, Perlman assumed that the client would learn ways of dealing with problems more effectively in the future. This emphasis on short-term, time-limited goals (Perlman, 1971) was subsequently reinforced by developments in crisis theory (such as Rapoport, 1962) and by research such as Reid and Shyne's (1969) which showed that short-term casework was more effective than long-term, open-ended treatment.

Problem-solving casework has two fundamental themes which are intended to operationalise social work's 'person-in-situation' tradition. As implied earlier, the first concerns the ways in which the client's motivation, capacity and/or opportunity to solve the problem are inadequate. The caseworker is directed to explore those aspects of the client's own personality that are involved in the problem, either as contributing causes or potential coping resources (Ripple, 1964). The second theme relates to the other persons and conditions operating in the problematic situation. Perl-man (1968) conceived of the client as living within a social 'role system', some part of which is probably impeding problem resolution. Thus, the caseworker seeks to under-stand the nature of the dysfunction or the breakdown in the client's role system. Because the problem-solving model views causation in a circular fashion, dysfunctional role systems are assessed both as a cause and a consequence of the presenting problem.

Permeating the notion of 'treatment' within the problem-solving framework is the constructive use of the relationship between worker and client. This is the continuous context within which problem-solving is said to take place. Clients are encouraged to reveal themselves to the caseworker, to start by exploring their feelings about the problem, their hopes for its resolution and their reactions to the present possibilities for resolution. The aim of this process is to encourage clients to want and use the means of helping that the agency, through the caseworker, makes available. It is as if the therapeutic relationship is used to socialise the client into the proper use of the agency (an orientation reminiscent of the functional school). After forming a sustaining relation-ship with the worker, clients are encouraged to go on and clarify their perception and understanding of the problematic situation, including their own role within it. Plans are made and monitored for clients to try out their capacities for solving the problem, material resources are mobilised, and linkages between clients and others are fostered with the aim of leading to the creation of more fulfilling social networks.

Notwithstanding the eclecticism of their thinking, Reid and Epstein's (Reid and Epstein, 1972; Epstein, 1980) pragmatic 'task-centred' approach properly belongs within the problem-solving tradition introduced to social work by Perlman. Reid and Epstein's is a somewhat more structured and system-atised model than Perlman's and the influences of systems theory and behavioural psychology are more pronounced but their underlying goals and assumptions are substantially the same. Like the problem-solving school, task-centred social work is also a way of helping people deal with problems in living. Clients are seen as rational people who, for one reason or another, are having trouble mobilising the necessary psychological, social or material resources to solve a particular problem. 'Treatment' is therefore a collaborative effort between client and worker in which the client's own problem-solving capacities are encouraged and stimulated. With the model, the first step is problem exploration and specification (a process that should take no more than one or two sessions). The aim is to come to a negotiated agreement on the problems to be dealt with in casework. The problems must be capable of precise specification and expressed in a language the client can understand. Client and worker also explore the context of the problem(s) in an effort to identify the contributing factors that are capable of manipulation by the worker and client together. From there, casework moves to formulate a contract in which the client agrees to work with the practitioner on one or more of the problems. The contract must specify objectives, milestones and the overall duration of treatment. Tasks are then planned for worker and client, with both parties agreeing to certain undertakings prior to each session. Where appropriate, incentives are built into the contract and the worker is directed to reinforce clients' progress and highlight benefits of their efforts which the clients may not have been aware of at the time. In planning each task, client and caseworker try to identify and make plans for dealing with obstacles. By simulating and rehearsing responses to these implementation difficulties it is hoped that clients will be forewarned and forearmed. Finally, the task-centred approach has prescriptions for terminating casework. Termination should have been anticipated from the outset when the objectives and termination date were set but, in the final interview, worker and client review progress and clients are either helped to plan how they will continue working on their tasks or else the problem-solving process is reviewed.

## The behavioural approach

The movement towards behaviour modification in social work marked by the publication of Thomas's (1967) collection of edited readings represents a fourth discernible tradition in casework theory. This approach assumes that problem behaviour is learned behaviour and therefore that behavioural disorders can be changed through strategic application of learning theory principles. Of course the theory and practice of behaviour modification were lifted straight out of experimental and clinical psychology where they had been under investigation for decades, but because so much of social casework at that time involved the alteration or stabilisation of client behaviour (Thomas, 1970), the techniques were eventually taken up by social workers eager for visible and speedy results. Many social workers found casework's earlier obsession with diagnosis and insight to be laborious and ineffective and, after the pioneering work of Perlman (1957) in the 1950s, the intellectual climate was ripe for the hard-headed empiricism of behavioural psychology.

As its name implies, behavioural casework focuses on observable responses without appeal to the kind of covert psychological processes underlying earlier casework methods. The basic questions during casework assessment are simply: what precise behaviours (including *outwardly discernible* thoughts and emotions) in the client and/or others involved in the situation need to be altered, and in what way(s)? Where possible a behavioural 'baseline' is established in which these behaviours are quantified prior to intervention, thereby setting the standard against which the successfulness of casework can ultimately be judged. Though not necessarily denying the importance of childhood experiences and previous learning in the aetiology of problem behaviour, behavioural caseworkers attempt to specify the internal and external (environmental) conditions which sustain the behaviour *now*. In other words, the caseworker must try to establish the pattern in the antecedents and consequences contemporaneous with the behaviour, under the assumption that these events are responsible for sustaining the problem behaviour.

A large part of behavioural casework's appeal lies in its straightforward and efficient treatment methods, an early summary of which appeared in a paper by Thomas (1968). In more recent times, Hudson and Macdonald (1986) have distinguished between four types of learning around which

a wide variety of treatment techniques developed. The first of these can be referred to as 'respondent techniques', derived from work in the area of Pavlovian or classical conditioning. The basic idea is that a previously neutral stimulus can come to evoke an 'unconditioned response' if it is paired with an 'unconditioned stimulus' often enough. An example of classical conditioning appears in the following chapter; dogs that had been continually subjected to painful electric shocks immediately after tones were sounded eventually came to fear the tone presented by itself. Research into classical conditioning of this kind spawned 'counterconditioning' procedures in which problem behaviour, such as a classically conditioned anxiety response, is diminished by continually pairing the feared stimulus with a new and competing response (in this case, relaxation). A second class of behavioural treatments can be called 'operant techniques' and these methods are based on the famous work of B. F. Skinner (cf. Skinner, 1971) who explored the laws governing behaviours which are strengthened by rewards and weakened by punishment or the absence of rewards (that is, operant behaviours). The techniques in this category include the use of positive reinforcement, negative reinforcement, extinction, punishment, differential reinforcement and response-shaping. Following the work of Bandura (1977) in social learning theory, casework began to make use of a third class of techniques inspired by the principles of observational learning. Most of these techniques make use of social skills training and rehearsal, in which problem situations are anticipated and potential coping responses are identified and rehearsed by the client before confronting the situation again in real life. Finally (and more recently), behavioural casework incorporates 'cognitive-behavioural techniques', which are based on the conviction that behaviour is not solely under the control of antecedents and consequences but that 'cognitions' or thoughts mediate between external stimuli and behaviour (Meichenbaum, 1978). For example, when confronted by threatening social situations, socially anxious individuals are said to engage in a kind of self-defeating internal dialogue that they may be only partly aware of, yet it is this dialogue which compounds, or even causes, their anxiety. Accordingly, cognitive behaviourists would seek to supplement whatever other behavioural techniques they might use by making the 'self-talk' explicit and calling on the client to examine the veracity of its content.

The four schools of thought discussed above were not, of course, the only intellectual movements within social case-work prior to the Generalist Era. Indeed, some of the early movements (often overlooked by radical critics) were much more socially progressive: for example, the social caseworker Bertha Reynolds (1951) was an outstanding social activist in the 1930s and 1940s who spent much of her career trying to integrate psychoanalysis with social reform. In addition, the crisis theory movement within social work (cf. Parad, 1965; Rapoport, 1962, 1970) mentioned in passing earlier was influential in its own right and has continued to develop into what is now a significant influence on social work practice (Panzer, 1983). Nevertheless, the psychosocial, functional, problem-solving and behavioural orientations were not only the most influential mainstream approaches of their day, but they continue to exert an influence on casework theory today.

*An assessment of pre-generalist approaches*

From a radical perspective, pre-generalist casework theory, irrespective of approach, contains at least four fundamental and interrelated flaws. All these issues will be elaborated on at various points throughout the remainder of this book so it will be sufficient to mention them only briefly at this point. First, the sole unit of concern – and the focus of all analysis – is the individual, even when so-called 'social factors' have been identified and targeted for intervention. By individua-lising client problems in this way, all the approaches reviewed so far are an obstacle to the development of a sense of class among clients. Radical casework, on the other hand, must foster the view among marginalised individuals that they are united with others in suffering problems which are sympto-matic of structural inequality. Second, the obvious emphasis in all the approaches is psychological change or develop-ment. Even those approaches which play down the notion of psychopathology nevertheless seek to correct deficiencies in the make-up of clients that are, to a greater or lesser extent, held responsible for the problems brought into casework. Third, all the approaches accept the prevailing social context as a given and seek only to work within current social arrangements. Social interventions are restricted to mobilising existing (remedial) resources or tinkering with the client's microsystem. The fourth problem follows from this, and it is that all the approaches have an extremely narrow understanding of what constitutes 'the social environment' or the 'in-situation' component of social work's 'person-in-situation' tradition. In all cases, the 'social environment' extends no further than the details of the client's immediate lifestyle. The more remote systems or structures responsible for setting the limits of their lives are ignored.

As we shall see, the present model does not deny the need for psychological change in clients, but that change is conceptualised as psychological empowerment. Moreover, our approach works towards uniting clients around shared problems and helping them to organise for change. Finally, as discussed in Chapter 1, our model makes use of an approach to casework assessment that fosters awareness of the structural causes of individual distress.

## The generalist era

It is frequently argued that social work is inherently generalist; that it has been generalist from the outset by virtue of its dual person and environment focus, for it is a focus which forces the practitioner to attend to factors ranging from individual needs to broad social policies and structures. It is a fact that the charity organisation societies from which professional social casework emerged in the United States in the late 1800s and early 1900s did concern themselves with issues of social justice and social policy (Pumphrey and Pumphrey, 1961). However, social work's perennial infatuation with professional status, coupled with the emergence of casework models that drew on advances within psychology, conspired to move practice towards a concentration on persons and a very circumscribed view of the environment. The so-called 'Hollis–Taylor Report' (E. V. Hollis and Taylor, 1951) recognised this trend and promulgated a 'multimethod' approach to practice which they believed would help social work to rediscover its generalist roots. As its name implies, multimethod practice requires that practitioners be familiar with casework, group work and community organisation. Although the statement was welcomed by many social work educators, it did not affect practice to any great extent.

More widely accepted and influential statements of generalist practice did not begin to emerge until the 1960s and 1970s, when radical social movements throughout the Western world inflamed criticism of casework for its reductionist approach to social problems. The search for generalist models was also fostered by the self-serving concern that fragmentation of social work into fields and methods of practice would weaken it industrially and professionally (Bartlett, 1970). Gordon (1965) and Bartlett (1970) formulated two of the earliest statements of a 'common base' for all social work practice, and the burden of their argument was that the social work perspective together with social work's purpose and values should direct the practitioner's activities. Theirs was essentially a case against 'the law of the instrument', which can be roughly translated as 'give a child a hammer and suddenly everything needs banging'. In other words, methods must not be allowed to define the nature of social work; rather methods should only be selected *after* a social work analysis of the case. As Teisiger (1983) has put it:

The appropriate starting point for interventions must be determined by an examination of the entire situation and not be framed by what is initially presented. The problem . . . selected for intervention will determine the methodology of choice rather than the methodological bias or expertise of the worker being used to define the problem. (p. 80)

In recent times there has been a proliferation of so-called generic practice models seeking to free social work from its bondage to methods (for example, Goldstein, 1973; Pincus and Minahan, 1973; Middleman and Goldberg, 1974; Siporin, 1975; Germain and Gitterman, 1980; Nelsen, 1980; Anderson, 1981; Meyer, 1983). Most of these models have at least two features in common: they assert the primacy of perspective over method, and they explicate a planned change process that is said to be common to all practice. Generic or generalist models make the assumption that social work has an eclectic theoretical base which is grounded in a systems framework for assessing multiple points of potential intervention. The worker is directed to assess all aspects of a situation with special emphasis on the client *system*, which may be an individual, a group, a community, or even an organisation. In addition to this, the generalist worker is supposed to be equipped with an understanding of the change process and a set of skills for facilitating this process at any and all system levels. Generally speaking, generic models describe the processes of change in terms of the following phases: (a) a problem exploration or assessment phase; (b) a contracting phase; (c) an intervention phase; (d) a monitoring and evaluation phase; and (e) a termination phase. The system(s) identified for change (the target system) in this process may or may not be the client system, and so general are some of the models that they effectively make no distinction at all between casework, group work or community work (for example, Pincus and Minahan, 1973; Germain and Gitterman, 1980).

While some would argue that we have now entered a post-generalist era in which the trend is towards a generalist–specialist hybrid (Brieland, 1987) and the re-emergence of specialist caseworkers, group workers and community workers, most writers would agree that specialties should be built on the kind of generalist base described. In other words, one's specialist contribution to a case must occur within a broader case analysis and intervention plan.

*An assessment of generalist approaches*

The basic problem with generalist models of practice is that they fail to distinguish between models *of* practice and models *for* practice. Whereas the role of the former is to describe practice, the role of the latter is to make prescriptions about how to practise. As descriptions or working definitions of practice, generalist models have been a much-needed development in thinking about social casework because they reinforced the social work commitment to holism and provided an identity which did not rely on the law of the instrument. But as models for practice generalist approaches are utterly inadequate. Anyone who has ever tried to use a generic model in practice knows that they are incapable of guiding action at any but the most general and obvious of levels. As models for practice most of them can be reduced to a series of fatuous propositions such as: think systemically; distinguish between clients and targets; an intervention must have a beginning a middle and an end. In seeking to be relevant to all presenting problems, generic models are relevant to none.

What is urgently needed now is theory development at a level beyond mere description. Social casework needs knowledge about *how* to intervene without diving back into the mire of reductionism from which it has been trying to emerge. While no theory or set of theories can tell caseworkers how to act in all situations, there is nevertheless a desperate need for practice models which develop strategies for operationalising the social work perspective.

In the previous chapter we presented a model *of* social casework which tries to remain true to the social work perspective. We must now move on to look at models *for* practice: that is, at some strategies, theories and tips for operationalising our model.

# 3

# A Psychology of Empowerment

Among the helping professions, social work has always had a unique relationship with marginalised and powerless members of society (Bailey and Brake, 1977; Simpkin, 1983). As so much of social work practice is conducted within public welfare bureaucracies, social work's clientele tends to contain two kinds of individual: those who lack the purchasing power to seek other solutions to their problems, and those who are constrained by the courts to submit to social work supervision. Common to both kinds of individual is a fundamental lack of control over some of the most important events in their lives. The term 'welfare recipient' is greatly disliked by social work practitioners, but it conveys a fundamental truth about the daily experience of being a social work client: it is an experience of dependency, of being a receiver. Indeed, the very institution of public welfare stands as a symbol to its clients of their powerlessness. This inescapable fact of social work practice is a crucial but greatly ignored consideration in the development of practice theory. It is not sufficient for casework theory merely to assert the client's right to self-determination; for most social work clients it is a case of discovering that even limited self-determination is *possible*. This brings us to the need for a psychology of empowerment on which to base casework practice.

Paulo Freire (1972a, 1972b) understood the importance of psychological empowerment in his work with the poor of South America. Born in an area of poverty and underdevelopment in Brazil in 1921, Freire experienced first-hand the psychological legacy of powerlessness. Although originally middle-class merchants, Freire's family was financially ruined by the pervasive pressures of the Great Depression that began in the United States in 1929. As a result, Freire came to know hunger and despair and to share listlessness and lethargy with the poor. Freire coined the term 'culture of silence' to refer to this apparent acceptance by the poor of their oppression. He concluded that the poor did not rise up and throw off their (American) oppressors because they were kept submerged by a process of cultural domination. In other words, the poor accepted their unhappy lot because they subscribed to an ideology of servitude which sanctioned their poverty and stifled criticism of the social order. As Freire once wrote:

> The dependent society is by definition a silent society. Its voice is not an authentic voice, but merely an echo of the voice of the metropolis – in every way the metropolis speaks, the dependent society listens. The silence of the object society in relation to the director society is repeated in the relationships within the object society itself. Its power elites, silent in the face of the metropolis, silence their own people in turn. (1970, p. 459)

Thus the 'dependence' Freire speaks of is not mere economic dependence, but a cultural and intellectual dependence which serves to subjugate the poor. Bound up in the culture of their oppression, marginalised members of society emulate the oppressor; they come to subscribe to the capitalist myth that we get what we deserve. As a result, they internalise the view that society has of them and, in the end, feelings of worthlessness and alienation possess them. In Freire's own terms, 'the oppressor lives inside'. Objectively, the poor have the greatest reason for social change but their subjective condition leaves them submerged and impotent.

Writing in a contemporary American context, the New Leftist author Michael Lerner (1979) coined the term 'surplus powerlessness' to capture the identical phenomenon in the working classes of the developed world. According to Lerner, over and above the actual powerlessness that the poor experience by virtue of being unable to control whole areas of their lives, there is the surplus powerlessness that they carry around with them like a script for living. Surplus powerlessness operates as a psychological legacy that cripples people and makes them believe that they can not change things; surplus powerlessness allows people to interpret their victories as defeats, to be cynical about whom they can trust and therefore reluctant to join with others in even small-scale political activity. Thus, like Freire, Lerner recognises the need for psychological change on the part of the poor. Surplus powerlessness is a psychological problem; certainly it has social roots, but social work theories which seek to avoid or deny the need for individual change are likely to be as inadequate as approaches which reduce all human problems to the level of psychopathology or behavioural disorder.

Though our explanations for it may differ, those who work closely with 'welfare recipients' know only too well what Freire and Lerner mean. We are accustomed to the passivity of our 'chronic' clients, even if we sometimes puzzle over their apparent lack of indignation. Apart from the rare outburst at trivial bureaucratic inefficiencies, most of our clients come to accept their lot and go through life making surprisingly few demands on a society which fundamentally excludes them. But how *can* caseworkers assist the poor to speak out rather than remain silent, to act for themselves rather than depend on others for meagre subsistence? In order to do this we must understand the psychological mechanisms responsible for silencing the poor in the first place.

**The psychological legacy of powerlessness**

The term 'learned helplessness' was first used approximately twenty years ago to describe the behaviour of mongrel dogs in a series of fear conditioning experiments. Since then the so-called 'learned helplessness effect' has been produced reliably in humans as well, and the psychological mechanism held responsible for the phenomenon is identical whether the behaviour is observed in dogs, humans or any other species. Moreover, the early dog experiments provide a useful (if rather sardonic) analogy for describing the lives of the poor.

In the early animal studies, Overmier and Seligman (1967) had intended to use a neutral tone in order to teach dogs shock-avoidance behaviour. The first step in their procedure involved conditioning the dogs to fear the tone. This part of the experiment followed the standard classical conditioning paradigm of restraining the dogs in a hammock and pairing the tone with a painful electric shock. It was expected that after fear conditioning, the tone could be used to motivate escape-avoidance behaviour in subsequent learning trials. In other words, because the dogs had come to fear the tone, they were expected to be quick to learn an escape-avoidance response when the tone was used to signal shock onset in future. On the contrary, however, most of the dogs given fear conditioning proved incapable of learning the response and after a few trials ceased responding altogether. Although they were surprised by this finding at first, Overmier and Seligman came to realise that the dogs had been desperately trying to escape the shock all along but, because the animals were restrained in hammocks, escape was simply not possible. Within the strict limits imposed on them, the dogs had tried everything they could and when nothing worked, they gave up trying. By the time escape was possible (during the learning trials) it was too late; the dogs had literally learned helplessness. Seligman, Maier and Geer (1968) later showed that the only way of teaching dogs that responding could indeed bring relief was by dragging them repeatedly across the barrier.

The learned helplessness hypothesis is the name given to the explanation offered by Maier, Seligman and Solomon (1969) and by Seligman, Maier and Solomon (1971) for the learned helplessness effect. According to this view, the dogs had been exposed to a situation during training in which the probability of an event (shock) occurring was identical whether they responded or not. In other words, the event was independent of the dog's behaviour, so by definition the situation was uncontrollable. And when an organism (animal or human) learns that an event and responding are independent of each other, the organism *learns helplessness* with respect to that event. Because they have not employed physically damaging stimuli, human helplessness experiments have been somewhat less dramatic than the early dog studies, but the processes involved are logically identical. Humans previously exposed to a stimulus they are unable to control also display deficits when attempting a new task, even if that task is quite dissimilar to the original, uncontrollable task (Hiroto and Seligman, 1975). Thus, both the human and animal studies reveal another important feature of the learned helplessness effect: that is, its capacity to generalise beyond the situation in which it originally developed.

Seligman (1975) has traced three steps in the development of learned helplessness. First, and most obviously, the person must be exposed to an uncontrollable event (one in which the outcome is independent of any action that can be taken). Second, information about the non-contingency between response and outcome must be processed and transformed into a cognitive representation of the situation. Seligman characterises this stage as the formation of an expectation or belief that responding is useless. This belief acts as a prediction about the future. The individual believes that the future will be just like the past; nothing can be done to change it. It is this expectation, not the objective situation, which is responsible for the breakdown of behaviour that is the third and final step in the process: learned helplessness.

Learned helplessness itself is a syndrome comprised of deficits in motivation, learning and emotion. The motivational deficit refers to perhaps the most visible feature of helplessness, the passive acceptance of suffering. The theory assumes that the incentive to respond in a traumatic situation is produced by the expectation that responding will produce relief. In the absence of this incentive, responding is likely to cease altogether and the helpless individual will virtually give up and lie down. It is this feature of learned helplessness that so troubled the young Paulo Freire.

The second feature of helplessness is essentially a cognitive problem and concerns the difficulty helpless people have in learning to reassociate actions and events in the future.

In other words, even if helpless individuals do manage to achieve things, they seem unable to see that it was *their* efforts that produced the outcome. Instead, they tend to invoke forces outside themselves (such as luck, or someone's generosity) to explain the situation. In this context it is significant that some of the helpless dogs in Overmier and Seligman's (1967) experiments actually emitted the correct response of jumping over the barrier in the shuttle box, but they did not benefit from the experience and failed to repeat the behaviour. This is a dramatic illustration of the cognitive feature of learned helplessness. Believing that events are uncontrollable interferes with the capacity to identify (and therefore to learn) coping responses even when the information is under one's very nose. And it is this feature of helplessness which Michael Lerner (1979) found so bewildering when the victories of the New Left during the 1960s and early 1970s failed to lead on to a radically new social order. As Lerner himself put it:

> The people who participated in these struggles did not gain a new sense of their own potential power. On the contrary, at the very moment when victories in the struggle were being won, activists redefined the criteria of success in such a way as to guarantee that they would end up being one down, in a way that would accentuate how little they had accomplished and how overwhelming were the tasks yet to be achieved. As a result, masses of people engaged in political activity in the 1960s were reconfirmed in their powerlessness. (p. 19)

It was as if they had learned nothing.

The third feature of helplessness occurs when uncontrollable events are subjectively important: that is, when the outcome really matters to us. Seligman (1975) holds that our first reaction to the possibility of an aversive outcome is fear, and fear is what motivates us to act. But once we form a belief in the inevitability or uncontrollability of the outcome, fear ceases to be functional and it gives way to resignation and despair. This kind of emotional emptiness is to be found everywhere our 'chronic' clients congregate: in hospital wards and psychiatric emergency rooms, in police stations and in jails, in welfare hostels, and in the back rooms of sympathetic relatives. It is the emotional cost of a life which has been directed by other people or fashioned by uncontrollable circumstances. Together these deficits form the syndrome of learned helplessness and Seligman (1972, 1975, 1978) was struck by the outward similarity between these deficits and the symptoms of depression. As a result, learned helplessness theory now proposes that the expectation that outcomes are independent of responses is a common mechanism underlying both conditions. Both learned helplessness and depression are said to have their roots in the belief that valued outcomes are uncontrollable.

In learned helplessness theory we therefore have the foundations for a psychology of powerlessness. The theory gives us an insight into the world of people who are regularly confronted by events beyond their control. The single parent reliant on welfare handouts for subsistence, the physically handicapped person who relies on others for the most basic human needs, the child exposed to erratic or abusive parenting, and the female victim of domestic violence are some of the powerless people caseworkers deal with. For powerless people like these choice is limited and control over valued outcomes resides with someone else. As a result they may come to accept the manifestly unacceptable and even renounce responsibility for themselves, leaving others to take initiatives on their behalf. These, then, are the 'silent' individuals and it is a *cognitive expectation* which is responsible for their silence; an expectation about the futility of action.

The early statement of learned helplessness theory was soon elaborated by several attribution theory reformulations (Abramson, Seligman and Teasdale, 1978; Miller and Norman, 1979; Roth, 1980), all of which seek to account for individual differences in the quality of helpless behaviour. After all, not everyone reacts to powerlessness in the same way. Some people never become helpless despite whatever grinding circumstances they must endure. In order to account for individual variation, helplessness theorists turned to the concept of causal attribution (cf. Heider,

1958). Essentially, learned helplessness theory now proposes that we need to understand how individuals explain the cause(s) of their circumstances before we can predict their reactions with any real accuracy. Thus, differences in causal attribution for helplessness determine differences in people's reactions.

The major attributional distinctions that have been drawn relate to the generality and chronicity of helplessness deficits as well as to the distinction between personal and universal helplessness. The distinction between personal and universal helplessness follows from the observation that some helpless individuals will come to believe that their own inadequacies are responsible for their helplessness, while others believe that anyone in their position would be similarly helpless. In those cases where individuals perceive personal helplessness, the theory predicts a decline in self-esteem in addition to the other helplessness deficits outlined above. The other major inadequacy of the old theory lies in its failure to specify boundary conditions. Given that the individual exposed to uncontrollable events does recognise the non-contingency and becomes helpless, the original theory makes no predictions as to how long the deficits will last (chronicity) or how widely they will generalise to other situations (globality). According to Abramson, Seligman and Teasdale (1978), when we realise we are helpless our instinctive reaction is to ask ourselves why, and the causal attribution we then make for helplessness determines these variables. The theoretical sequence now becomes:

Objective noncontingency → Perception of present and past noncontingency → Attribution for present and past noncontingency → Expectation of future noncontingency → Symptons of helplessness.
(Abramson, Seligman and Teasdale, 1978, p. 52)

The authors proposed three causal dimensions as being most salient in mediating the three variable qualities of helplessness. First, the generality of helplessness deficits is said to be determined by the globality versus specificity of the causal attribution (thus globality and specificity are opposite poles of a continuum with the actual attribution occurring at or between the extremes). Similarly, the chronicity of helplessness deficits is said to depend on the stability versus transience of the causal attribution, and the effect of helplessness on self-esteem relies on the internality versus externality of one's attribution. Generally speaking, then, the reformulated learned helplessness model contends that helplessness will be most severe when causal attributions for powerlessness involve global, stable and internal factors. For example, unemployed people who blame their lack of ability for repeated failures to find work are invoking an internal, stable, global cause and are likely to suffer much greater distress in a wider range of situations than people who blame temporary fluctuations in economic circumstances (an external, unstable, specific cause).

It must be stressed that under both the original and reformulated theories it is the expectation that no action will control outcomes in the future that is the sufficient condition for learned helplessness. What has been said so far concerns variations in the quality of helplessness deficits. But the concept of causal attribution has also been invoked to account for how it is that some powerless people resist becoming helpless at all. According to Peterson and Seligman (1984), individuals adopt a general *attributional style* or predisposition to explain events in a certain way and this attributional style either predisposes or immunises individuals to helplessness. Individuals who tend to invoke internal, stable and global factors (such as 'I'm incompetent') for negative events, and external, unstable and global factors for positive events (such as 'I was just lucky') suffer in two ways. First, they are predisposed to becoming helpless when exposed to events they can not control and, second, their causal attribution for being helpless exacerbates the psychological deficits that ensue. How it is that individuals develop such an insidious attributional style in the first place has not been addressed by learned helplessness theorists but there is some evidence (cf. Feather and Barber, 1983) that repeated exposure to uncontrollable events may be sufficient in itself for individuals to develop a depressive attributional style. If so, this must surely be the most unjust consequence of powerlessness, and one which explains why some battered women, for example, eventually come to blame themselves for their plight.

## Casework with the powerless

As social workers, we are accustomed to critics of the welfare state accusing 'welfare recipients' of 'doing nothing to help themselves'. But from what is now known about the psychology of powerlessness, the wonder is that anything else should be expected. It is true that powerlessness breeds passivity; but this is not the same thing as laziness or apathy. It is more likely that those poor and 'chronic' clients who actually do shun responsibility have reached the conclusion that nothing they try to do for themselves will work. Accordingly, casework with the weak requires tactics for challenging passivity without blaming those who display it.

It was shown earlier that there are two critical moments in the development of helpless behaviour. The first is exposure to uncontrollability, and the second is the formation of a cognitive expectation that responding is useless. Seeking opportunities to reverse these experiences should alleviate or even remove helplessness deficits altogether. Reversing the first of these critical moments obviously involves exposing the client to as many controllable events as possible. The general strategy should be to help powerless individuals identify those important areas of their lives over which they already do exercise control as well as those areas where it is possible to exercise greater control. This tactic can involve worker and client in negotiations with other individuals and even other welfare agencies aimed at maximising the client's power in the relationship. If successfully implemented, this 'environmental enrichment' tactic should result in the client recognising that some valued outcomes can be attained and some potentially negative outcomes avoided by him- or herself. While many important life events can never be controlled by the poor because of their lack of resources, caseworkers must seize every opportunity to expose their clients to outcomes that *are* controllable. If nothing else, we may succeed in preventing helplessness learned in one situation from generalising to other situations. In this context it is important to remember that the worker him- or herself is a significant part of the client's social environment and the relationship between client and worker will inevitably mitigate or compound helplessness in the client. It is lamentably common for social workers to reinforce the power differential that exists between them and their clients. Workers who make unilateral decisions about when, where and even *if* their clients can see them, for example, do so at a cost to the client. Similarly, the administrative procedures adopted by social work agencies often have the effect of frustrating or confusing clients and thereby confirming them in the view that power over their lives lies elsewhere.

It follows from our earlier discussion of learned helplessness theory that mere exposure to controllable events is unlikely to be enough however. Recall that in the early animal studies the motivational deficit which followed uncontrollable shock was so severe that the experimenters had to force the animals to respond, and the cognitive deficit was such that this tactic had to be repeated many times before the animals learned that responding would work. Similarly, those who work with the poor must be prepared to coax their clients into action and not (as the social work tradition of client self-determination tends to imply) always wait for the client to take the initiative. Moreover, once action has been taken and control experienced, it may be necessary to spend time with clients ensuring they actually perceive the control they have exercised. Finally, the process will need to be repeated over and over before powerless individuals begin to anticipate greater control in the future. As Michael Lerner (1979) discovered during the radical movements of the 1960s, the odd victory will be interpreted as an isolated and purely fortuitous event.

Given the significance of attributional processes in the development of helplessness deficits, our casework methods should also include attending to the way clients explain life events to themselves. In order to minimise the psychological effects of powerlessness, workers need to watch for certain qualities of the client's general attributional style as well as for specific attributions occurring during the casework process. Specifically, and to the extent that reality permits, attributions for undesirable life events (such as domestic violence) should be moved in the direction of externality, instability and/or specificity to avoid self-blame and unjustified generalisation. Conversely, attributions for positive events should be moved in the direction of internality, stability and/or globality to maximise the potential psychological benefits of the experience. Central to the emerging area of feminist counselling is the recognition that oppressed women do require help in making realistic attributions for their successes as well as for their problems and there is a growing literature devoted to this issue. In her work with depressed house-bound women, for example, Layden (1982) asked her clients to keep a diary of all the happy and unhappy events of the week. The women were also required to identify all (and only) the external reasons for the unhappy times and all the possible internal reasons for the happy times. At the end of the week this exercise was reinforced by group sessions in which the women came together to share and confirm the adaptive attributions they had made.

Fosterling (1985) has identified a number of other strategies for modifying causal attributions, some of which could be used as a focus for counselling or simply as tips for guiding the discussions that occur in the context of more limited or task-centred casework. These strategies include using social reinforcement (praise) for appropriate causal attributions that emerge in the course of conversation, using persuasion via modelling and group pressure (see Layden, 1982), and confronting clients with information which is incompatible with their existing (negative) attributional style. Although not specifically designed for attributional change, the cognitive therapy tactics of Beck and his colleagues (Beck, 1967; Beck *et al.*,1979) also provide us with workable casework methods for mitigating helplessness. Beck required his clients to record their thoughts whenever they were confronted by emotionally troublesome experiences. The focus of counselling then became the 'automatic thoughts' elicited by these events that were responsible for producing unhappiness and passivity. The client was challenged to evaluate the reasonableness of the thoughts, with the caseworker acting as a kind of scientific collaborator in the exercise. The evidence for and against the client's attribution was dispassionately evaluated and alternative explanations for events were advanced. One of the potential advantages of Beck's technique is that much of the work is done outside counselling so the procedure can be used either as an adjunct to casework or as the focus of casework itself. If the former, the worker could spend a few minutes before the main business of each session reviewing the client's week and helping to evaluate the plausibility of the client's attributions for events. There is considerable evidence that this rather simple discipline will eventually move general attributional style in the desired direction (for example, Murphy *et al.*, 1984; Teasdale, 1985).

As we shall see, the goal of empowering clients psychologically is fundamental to the present model of practice. If we are successful in this, not only will we have helped individual clients become more assertive and self-directed but we will have laid the groundwork for the later stages of our model. For clients to join with others in pressing for social reform, they must be convinced that their efforts will bear fruit. In mounting the kind of campaign we will discuss in Chapters 6 and 7 there is no room for learned helplessness, and the process of eroding this psychological legacy of powerlessness must begin during casework.

Before discussing the transition from casework to community organisation it is necessary to discuss one other characteristic of casework practice. Arguably it is the one which causes social workers in public welfare the most discomfort: namely, our role as agents of social control with involuntary clients and how this can be reconciled with the goal of empowering our clients.

# 4

# A Slight Digression: Casework with Involuntary Clients

Despite the recognition in at least some of the social work practice literature (for example, Pincus and Minahan, 1973; Compton and Galaway, 1984) that relationships between workers and clients need not always be harmonious to be constructive, social work continues to train its students almost exclusively in interviewing skills that are more appropriate to voluntary (and often white middle-class) clients. A great deal of effort is devoted to achieving a proper 'helping relationship' in which clients are encouraged to explore the problem and come to a resolution in their own way and in their own time. Keith-Lucas (1972), for example, considers that the helping relationship can be defined as 'the medium which is offered to people in trouble through which they are given the opportunity to make choices, both about taking help and the use they will make of it' (p. 47). He goes on to proclaim that concern for the client dictates that the worker should be willing 'to let the helped person decide to what extent and under what conditions he [sic] is willing to be helped'. Concern for the client, according to Keith-Lucas,

> does not mean necessarily agreeing to help under these circumstances, or even refraining from pointing out that help is not possible under them. Nor does it mean refraining from offering what help is available, or even, if

the need is desperate, intervening in an attempt to get help started. But it does mean, ever and always, treating the helped person as the subject of the sentence, serving his interest, allowing him all possible freedom to be what he wants to be. (p. 103)

This concern for client self-determination translates into casework practices that stress empathy and nondirectiveness. Much of the social work literature on interviewing behaviour is derivative of work within counselling psychology, especially of writers like Rogers (1951, 1957, 1961, 1967, 1975) and Carkhuff (1969a, 1969b; Carkhuff and Berensen, 1976; Carkhuff and Anthony, 1979) and others within this tradition (such as Ivey, 1983; Egan, 1985). These writers believe fervently in unconditional acceptance of the client by the worker and in the development of an alliance between worker and client. According to Rogers there are certain 'core conditions' which are necessary to produce therapeutic change in the client. First, the therapist must be a congruent, genuine, integrated person: that is, the therapist must avoid presenting a façade or denying his or her own reactions to the events that occur during counselling. Second, the therapist must convey an attitude of 'unconditional positive regard'; the client is valued unconditionally, without regard to his or her behaviour. Third, the therapist must strive to achieve empathy, or the capacity to sense and understand the client's private world as if it were the worker's own. As well as these core conditions, Rogers claimed that a relationship between client and worker had to exist, that client and worker had to *matter* to each other so that each 'makes some perceived difference in the experiential field of the other' (Rogers, 1967, p. 46). Finally, the client had to be 'in a state of incongruence, being vulnerable and anxious' about the problem. In other words, the client must *own* the problem and genuinely wish to change. For years counselling psychologists have continued to view these qualities as fundamental to the helping relationship. The influential author Gerard Egan (1985), for example, stresses that the worker must convey 'respect' for the client, an attitude which he defines as being '*for*' the client, and of regarding the client as unique, with a right to self-determination, possessed of goodwill and a genuine desire to work on the problem.

Generally speaking, social work educators have been uncritical in their application of this literature to practice. Almost every introductory text on social work practice devotes considerable attention to methods for creating the right 'helping' relationship. To take just one example Hepworth and Larsen (1986), consider that the establishment of 'rapport' is the first task facing the social worker in casework; without rapport, they assert, intervention is doomed from the outset. To Hepworth and Larsen, establishing rapport requires being able to operationalise the following: '(1) non-judgmental attitude, (2) acceptance, (3) clients' right of self-determination, and (4) respect for clients' worth and dignity, uniqueness and individuality, and problem-solving capacities. And finally, practitioners foster rapport when they relate with *empathy* and *authenticity*' (pp. 26–7).

The problem with the unqualified importation of counselling psychology methods into social work is that much of social work practice cannot be considered therapeutic in the narrow psychological sense of that term. It follows that the formation of a relationship which aims to facilitate (psycho)therapeutic change may be neither fundamental nor even desirable in certain circumstances. Nowhere is this clearer than in the case of the involuntary client. With clients whose sole reason for social work contact is because of external constraint, the very foundations are knocked out from under the 'helping relationship'. How realistic is it to assume that the client is motivated to solve the problem when he or she may not even accept that a problem exists? What sort of mental gymnastics is required to convey unconditional positive regard and a belief in client self-determination when the very relationship between worker and client may mean the difference to the client between freedom and imprisonment? As discussed in an earlier chapter, social workers are predominantly involved with public welfare recipients and many of these are at best reluctant, and at worst hostile, recipients of social work services. To the regret of many practitioners, we simply can not apply the comfortable, middle-class assumptions of our psychologist colleagues when working with such people.

In the Australian state of Victoria in 1986, 60 per cent of all public child-care workers resigned, and in at least one regional office every single worker left in this twelve-month period. And 1986 was not an unusual year; resignations have proceeded at this rate for years, with the result that many positions are unfilled and morale amongst those who remain is chronically low. The reasons for this despair are many and complex but some of the blame must be laid at the feet of social work educators. State child care workers spend a great deal of their time working with resistant parents who submit to social work intervention under pain of losing their children, yet most graduates are totally unprepared for dealing with such people. All too often the intervention plan breaks down at the beginning, at the stage of engagement, because current practice models encourage social workers to approach the client from a therapeutic viewpoint. But when all the polite, non-directive responses run out, as eventually they must, the worker becomes discouraged and gives up.

Work with involuntary clients must begin with the recognition that the interaction between worker and client is based on *conflict* rather than cooperation, that social work with involuntary clients is a *political*, not a therapeutic, process involving the socially sanctioned use of power. The political nature of this activity becomes obvious when one calls to mind what it means to be an involuntary client in the first place; by definition, the sole or primary reason for receiving social work intervention is because 'the client's' behaviour is considered by someone else to be deviant or troublesome while the client him- or herself resists the intervention at some level. Indeed, the involuntary recipient of social work services is not usually the client at all as the ultimate beneficiary of the work done will be those who in some way suffered from the 'client's' aberrant behaviour in the first place.

Thus involuntary casework is a threat to one of the most cherished human desires – freedom – and Rooney (1988) has recently reminded social workers that the likely response to this threat is reactance behaviour. The term 'reactance' was first coined by the social psychologist, Brehm (1972), who used it to describe the resistance individuals put up when they are confronted with a possible loss of freedom. According to Brehm, individuals who have an expectation of being able to control a certain outcome or event will respond to the loss of control with a heightened level of arousal that translates into motivation to restore freedom. The threatened individual will not passively accept the situation but will engage in whatever behaviours he or she thinks are appropriate to re-exert control. The strength of this reactance behaviour is a function both of the importance of the valued freedom and the client's expectation of being able to control the event. Individuals who are more accustomed to controlling important events in their lives can therefore be expected to show greater reactance behaviour when they perceive a potential loss of control by submitting to casework. In a real sense, then, reactance is adaptive behaviour which is driven by the desire to control one's own life. The hostility of our more assertive involuntary clients may be a problem for social workers but it is an indication of some psychological resilience in our involuntary clients. Indeed, in a recent revision of reactance theory, Wortman and Brehm (1975) have argued that reactance behaviour will only last for so long; if all avenues of self-control are closed, reactance will eventually give way to learned helplessness. Helpless clients may be more compliant but, as we saw in the previous chapter, there is no sense in which their behaviour can be considered adaptive. Here, then, is the social worker's dilemma: how should we approach involuntary casework with a resistant client, given that some level of reactance is adaptive and yet some level of cooperation is indispensable if anything at all is to be achieved?

Assuming the worker is prepared to undertake the work in the first place, social workers engaged in involuntary casework have three broad practice options open to them. The first and, because of our current practice models, most common reaction is to bury the political dimension of the work and avoid conflict wherever possible. Against all the odds, workers committed to this approach will persist in the quest for affirmation and warmth. They are likely to feel uncomfortable, even apologetic, about the constraints on the client and will make all kinds of concessions in an effort to reduce client hostility and mitigate the impact involuntarism. We can refer to this attempt to buy cooperation as '*casework by concessions*' and it can often be observed among inexperienced and idealistic practitioners who express their commitment to clients by deferring to them wherever possible. However, because conflict of interests is intrinsic to the involuntary relationship, concessions can extend only so far before the worker must eventually call a halt to the process and stamp his or her authority on the relationship. Thus attempts to appease involuntary clients through concessions are likely to leave both worker and client bitter and resentful: the worker because he or she will be forced to go out further and further on a limb, and the client because, inevitably, a point will be reached where he or she is subjugated again anyway.

A second and antithetical casework option can be referred to as '*casework by oppression*'. Under this approach the worker accepts, even embraces, the conflict and fights hard to ensure that his or her terms are complied with. Here the worker makes no pretence to the 'helping relationship' and has no compunction whatever about browbeating the client. No doubt because of the revulsion most workers feel towards domestic violence, violent male clients are often treated in this way. From the outset they are told by the worker exactly what they can and cannot do and what will happen to them if they do not comply. While it is true that involuntarism inevitably places limits on the client's behaviour which must be clear from the outset, workers who set uncompromising and unilateral terms in their relationship are often guilty of trying to punish the client under the guise of social work practice. Whatever may be said about the justice of punishment, this quite clearly is not the social worker's role.

In this chapter we will consider a third casework option. While this approach avoids mere acquiescence to client demands, it asserts that the alternative need not be outright oppression. The approach assumes that it is possible to strive for client empowerment even while acting as an agent of social control. The two roles may be in tension but they need not be contradictory. A degree of reconciliation is possible through the adoption of the role of *negotiator* or *conflict manager*. The remainder of this chapter is devoted to a discussion of the 'casework by negotiation' option.

## Negotiated casework

As previously discussed, the place for the worker to start with involuntary clients is with his or her own perception of the situation. In place of the spurious assumptions of the therapeutic approach, workers must accept the political nature of their work and the conflict of interests that exists between them and their clients. This conflict should be made explicit by the worker at the outset and ways must be found to ensure that *both* parties emerge with as many as possible of their interests being met. In place of a 'helping' relationship, then, the foundation of social casework with involuntary clients is a 'working' relationship wherein client and worker are prepared to work towards a speedy resolution of the problem and reinstatement of the client's liberty.

The aim of negotiation is threefold. First, negotiation is a means of identifying opportunities for maximising client self-determination within the constraints under which casework is conducted. Second, negotiation engages the client in the process of operationalising the order responsible for casework in the first place, rather than merely forcing the client to submit to a plan which has been entirely worked out by others. By involving the client in the intervention plan, it is likely that there will be less resistance to change and a more rapid resolution of the problem. Finally, the behaviour of skilled negotiators serves as a model to involuntary clients of peaceful conflict resolution. Many individuals become involuntary clients because they have sought to impose their wishes on unwilling victims through force, so the acquisition of more reasoned and peaceful problem-solving methods is likely to have benefits far beyond the immediate situation.

Negotiated casework involves the following steps:

1. clear the air;
2. identify legitimate client interests;
3. identify non-negotiable aspects of intervention;
4. identify negotiable aspects of intervention;
5. negotiate the case plan;
6. agree on criteria for progress.

In the sections that follow, each of these steps will be discussed in turn.

*Step one: clearing the air*

Where the client submits to casework because of a court order, or the threat of a court order, the social worker symbolises the full might of the legal system and at least to begin with the worker will have no identity other than oppressor. Under such circumstances, all the social worker's communications will be filtered through a haze of distrust, suspicion and hostility. This haze must be cleared away and channels of communication opened up for any progress to be made.

To begin the process, the worker should direct the client's attention to the order that brings them together. Where applicable, it can be useful to bring a copy of the court order to the first meeting and read it through with the client. This not only sets the terms of the relationship but it stands as a symbol of the third party (the court) which is ultimately responsible for the limits placed on the worker's and the client's behaviour. While the worker should anticipate, or even invite, some expression of antipathy in the early stages, it is important that the conflict not be allowed to degenerate into a personal dispute between the two parties. In a very real sense, the social worker's role is to negotiate a settlement between the client and the court and it is important that this be plain from the outset; it is *not* a dispute between worker and client but between the client and *society at large*. If this is not clear to the client, then the worker's capacity to relate to the client will be made that much more difficult.

This is not to suggest that the worker should apologise for his or her work or seek to dispense with client resentment by hiding behind the court order. Indeed, after restating the terms of the order, the worker should invite the client's reaction. The kind of empathic responses advocated in the counselling literature become appropriate at this point. Open-ended questions such as, 'How do you feel about the court's decision?' should then be asked, and any feelings of resentment in the client explored. The inherent ambiguity in the relationship between worker and client should also be discussed at this point. Statements, such as 'You must feel pretty reluctant to work with me under these circumstances' can open the way to a frank and full discussion of the relationship. It should be remembered that not all involuntary clients will harbour ill-will towards the worker; some will be eager to work on the problem that brought them into the hands of the law. Despite the court order, it would be incorrect to describe such individuals as involuntary clients and more traditional casework methods may be appropriate for them.

Although drawing on counselling skills to foster discussion, the worker must avoid lapsing into the bland detachment of the psychotherapist. Whereas in psychotherapy it may be quite appropriate for the worker to convey an attitude of benign impartiality, in involuntary work, this kind of detachment is both artificial and dishonest. The involuntary client's problem is not entirely personal; the worker is an intrinsic part of it. As previously stated, 'the problem' is a conflict of interests between the client and others whose interests are represented by the social worker. Moreover, the unwillingness of the 'therapeutic' worker to self-disclose simply reinforces the power differential between worker and client by insulating the worker from the same personal risks that are demanded of the client. Like any party in any disagreement, the worker should be prepared to enter fully into discussion of the problem to which he or she is a party. Where applicable, this means disclosing his or her own discomfort in the relationship, fears about the outcome of the work, constraints under which he or she is operating, and so on. Obviously, the worker's expression of feeling must be tempered with commonsense and respect for the client; the client should not be blamed for the worker's predicament or prevented from exploring his or her own feelings because the worker's reactions dominate proceedings.

In summary, then, step one in the involuntary casework process involves setting the stage for negotiation by restating the order under which casework is being conducted, encouraging the client to air his or her feelings about the situation and allowing the worker to emerge as a real and active participant in the problem; one who is in the position of mediator between the court and the client.

*Step two: identify legitimate client interests*

When client and worker have expressed their feelings about the situation, the negotiation process can proceed to the next stage, that of identifying the *reasons* for client resistance. The ultimate aim of this step is to list the legitimate client interests that appear to be threatened by the social work intervention. Thus the focus of attention is not so much what needs to be achieved before casework can be terminated, as what lies behind the client's objection to casework in the first place.

Very often the difficulty experienced by social workers in working with involuntary clients arises because intervention plans are decided upon prematurely. When the worker can see only one way of executing a court order the major task ahead can only be to ensure that the client complies. However, although there will obviously be non-negotiable components of a court order, there is usually some part of the casework plan that is open to negotiation, and much of the art of involuntary work boils down to creating as much freedom of choice as possible within the limits that apply.

To avoid foreclosing on the intervention plan, then, the worker needs to know with considerable clarity just what the client stands to lose by submitting to casework. In the beginning this may not be clear even to clients themselves; they tend to be so preoccupied with the *fact* that their freedom is limited that they fail to explore how their lives will actually be diminished. The more assertive clients may tell us that they want nothing to do with us or with the system we represent but, short of restating this position over and over, they are often unable to tell us what their objection is based on. The general rule in this situation is for the worker to *look behind the client's position to the interests that he or she is fighting to protect.* Once individuals have been given ample opportunity to express their hostility at becoming involuntary clients, the worker should invite them to explain exactly what they stand to lose. This question moves the negotiation process one level deeper and prevents the interview degenerating into mere restatement of opposition.

Clearly the most fundamental interest that will be threatened is the client's right to self-determination and just as clearly this is a legitimate interest which the worker should not only help make explicit but, as we shall see, should also take seriously when formulating intervention plans. As well as this very basic and very general objection to involuntarism, however, there will usually be a number of secondary interests that are threatened by social work intervention. Secondary objections may be as broad as not wanting to be seen to need professional help, or as specific as wishing to avoid the cost of transport to the agency. Once again, these are legitimate objections which need to be identified and respected: for example, the case plan may stipulate procedures that ensure significant others are not made aware of the situation, or provide for the worker to call at the client's house rather than force the client to incur the cost of transport.

*Step three: identify non-negotiable aspects of intervention*

As emphasised throughout this chapter, involuntary work must be based on an honest admission of the conflictual nature of the relationship. Anything less is not only self-defeating, it is ultimately dishonest. Accordingly, while step two is designed to open up possibilities for case planning, our next step must be to clarify what (if any) aspects of the plan cannot be compromised.

By this time in the casework process, quite an effort has already gone into establishing the 'working relationship' referred to earlier and by now at least some of the client's hostility should have been dealt with. For this reason it can be useful for the worker to change seating position when he or she enters step three of the negotiation process. Whereas in the earlier discussion it was appropriate to symbolise the conflict by sitting square on to the client, one's willingness to work together with the client can be expressed at this point by drawing one's chair alongside the client so as to study the order together. Where possible, a copy of the order (where one exists) should be placed on a desk or table so that both worker and client can sit side-by-side throughout this step.

To the extent that reality permits, specific directives can be reframed by the worker to make them more consistent with the interests identified by the client in step two. For example, any probationer will naturally be anxious to avoid the police as much as possible, so in reading through the conditions of probation, the worker might reframe a clause such as, 'The probationer is required to attend as and when required', to something like, 'The police will leave you alone as long as we keep in regular contact'. But however they are phrased, step three only ends when worker and client agree on precisely what conditions are not open to negotiation.

It should be stressed that step three is not always as straightforward as it might appear at first. Since workers can frequently see only one way of executing an official directive, they may consign more to the realm of 'non-negotiable' than is justified. For example, the non-negotiable component of the probation order referred to above is only that worker and client must keep in contact; everything else including time, place, method and frequency is potentially negotiable. However, workers and clients are inclined to draw certain (usually self-serving) conclusions about what is implicit in court orders like this one, and for this reason it is most important that both parties be prepared to question their interpretations of all clauses and agree on the precise behaviours that form the 'bottom line'. The aim of this exercise is twofold. First, it sets the inevitable limits of negotiation and so prevents the kind of self-destructive 'casework by concessions' approach outlined at the outset. Second, by examining and eliminating needless assumptions

about what is implied in each clause of the order, the process
of empowering the involuntary client is begun.

*Step four: identify potentially negotiable aspects of
intervention*

Having agreed on the non-negotiable components of social
work intervention and so set the parameters within which
compromise is possible, the next step is to identify all
possible clauses in the case plan whose negotiation can be
left to the worker and client. As we shall see, some of the
skills required to undertake this task successfully are the
antithesis of those required in step three. Whereas in step
three worker and client are engaged in a process of careful
definition requiring precision, attention to detail and careful
scrutiny of presuppositions, step four requires creativity and
imagination as well. Worker and client now think as broadly
as they can about the situation in an effort to generate as
many life domains as possible over which the client can
exercise some freedom of choice.

To achieve this breadth of coverage, it can be useful to
employ the following structured problem-solving procedure.
The first step in the procedure is to *define the problem at
hand*. The issue requiring negotiation should be stated
specifically and concretely: for example, following their
discussion of all non-negotiable elements of a probation
order, probationer and probation officer would now restate
the clause, 'The probationer must attend as and when
required', and address the question, 'Given that we must
keep in contact, what aspects of this contact can we
legitimately negotiate about?' Thus, agreed on what constitutes the bottom line of the involuntary order, the parties
involved in the intervention plan now pose questions about
what else is required to complete the planning.

Having defined the negotiable issues, the next step in the
problem-solving procedure is to 'brainstorm' the possibilities
for each. There are four basic rules to keep in mind when
brainstorming (cf. Osborn, 1963). The first is that criticism is
not allowed. In other words, neither of the parties is
permitted to criticise any of the ideas until later. Second,

the wilder the idea, the better. The reasoning behind this rule being that it is easier to reject ideas later than it is to have the ideas in the first place. Third, quantity is the goal because the greater the number of ideas generated, the more likely it is that all possibilities will actually be canvassed. Finally, combination and improvement are desirable, (that is, as well as contributing ideas of their own, participants are free to propose ways of improving the suggestions of others or of combining some of the ideas together). According to D'Zurilla and Goldfried (1971) there are two basic principles behind Osborn's (1963) brainstorming rules: (a) deferment of judgement and (b) quantity breeds quality. The first of these principles is based on the premise that if a person begins the process of evaluating or censoring ideas while supposedly generating ideas, creativity will be stifled and potentially good solutions will be overlooked. Instead, discussion will become bogged down in the merits of whatever ideas are had first. The second principle – quantity breeds quality – follows from the first and is based on the simple statistical reality that the more ideas one generates, the more likely one is to arrive at the best solution to the problem.

In keeping with the aims of creativity and quantity of ideas, it can be useful to invite others to participate in the brainstorming session, provided that these others are acceptable to the client and not perceived by him or her as opposed to his or her interests.

*Step five: construct the case plan*

The next step in the negotiation process is where the details of the intervention plan are decided upon. The aim is to decide upon and combine all the negotiable components of the plan identified in step three with the non-negotiable components identified in step two. By the end of step three, all that has been agreed is what is potentially negotiable in the intervention plan. No decisions have yet been made about the terms of the agreement itself. Thus, for example, step three would conclude when probationer and probation officer agree that time, place, method and frequency of contact are all potentially negotiable aspects of the casework plan. Now, in step four, the aim is to make decisions about all these issues. To facilitate the process it can be useful if a written list of client interests has been produced during step two of the negotiation. This list can now be used to guide decisions about specific clauses of the intervention plan.

Also at this point it is appropriate for the worker to declare his or her own legitimate interests in the casework relationship. Naturally the worker will want some say in when, how, where and how often he or she meets with the client, and now is the time to declare what interests the worker has in decisions about such matters. It must be stressed that we are talking here about the *interests* that will form the basis of case planning decisions, not about the decisions themselves. For the worker to suggest, for example, that one of his or her interests is not to meet outside the agency is to confuse an interest with a position. In this case there is clearly no scope for negotiation about where to meet because the worker has pre-empted the decision. Where the worker is truly determined to meet at the agency, it would be preferable (though unfortunate) to identify this as another of the non-negotiable aspects of intervention back at Step Two. However, assuming the worker is at least open to the possibility of meeting elsewhere, the legitimate interest that lies behind his or her reluctance to do so may be the wish to avoid lengthy travel time in supervising the client.

When all potentially negotiable components of the case plan have been identified and all legitimate interests have been declared, the way is clear for the worker and client to seek agreement on casework terms that satisfy as many as possible of the interests of both parties. The problem-solving skills outlined in step four will again be useful as creative solutions will be necessary: for example, in decisions about where to meet, the worker may need to pose the problem, 'Where can we meet so that you are spared transport costs (client interest) and I am spared extensive travel time (worker interest)?' Brainstorming may reveal venues other than the agency or the client's residence, or the possibility of worker or client combining supervision visits with other business in the area, or of taking it in turns to travel to the other's preferred venue, and so on.

Naturally this process is likely to throw up more than one possibility for each potentially negotiable aspect of the case plan, so some means for choosing between possibilities is necessary. The basic aim must be to choose the option which satisfies as many of the client's and the worker's legitimate interests as possible. In other words, the best option is the one that is *fairest* to both parties, and fairness can be determined by how the option relates to the legitimate interests of worker and client. Where an option is a direct negation of one or more of a party's interests, it must be considered unfair to that party. This is not to deny the inevitability of compromise in the negotiation process, but simply to assert that the ultimate criteria for judging fairness are the interests identified in step two: the fairest options are those which optimise the interests of both parties.

Where agreement is difficult to reach, a simple but useful aid is a modification of Janis and Mann's (1977) so-called 'decisional balance sheet' (see Figure 4.1). The aim of this procedure is to ensure that the parties to the decision give careful consideration to all the likely consequences of the various courses of action open to them. Janis and Mann distinguish between 'utilitarian' consequences and 'approval' consequences. As the term implies, utilitarian considerations refer to all the expected instrumental effects of the decision with regard to self and significant others. For example, when choosing among several possible venues for contact between worker and client, the client will take account of utilitarian considerations such as distance from home, availability of transport, cost of transport options, and so on. Approval considerations, on the other hand, refer to the internalised moral standards of oneself and others. These considerations include the feelings of shame or pride that may accompany one option or the other, as well as the potential approval or disapproval that the various courses of action will attract from significant others. Although approval considerations may not be involved in every decision, it is important that the question at least be asked. Thus, for each alternative under consideration, the following decisional balance grid would be completed for both worker and client.

|                                                             | Positive consequences | Negative consequences |
| ----------------------------------------------------------- | --------------------- | --------------------- |
| Tangible gains and losses for self                          |                       |                       |
| Tangible gains and losses for others (including the other party) |                  |                       |
| Self-approval or disapproval                                |                       |                       |
| Approval or disapproval of significant others               |                       |                       |

**Figure 4.1**   *An adaptation of Janis and Mann's 'decisional balance sheet'*

Although it is best that separate decisional balance grids are completed for both worker and client, there is no reason for them not to confer. Before moving to select the option that satisfies the greatest number of utilitarian and approval gains, both worker and client should identify the most important of the considerations nominated in the grid. Worker and client should go back over their grids and isolate which of the factors are the most attractive to them. The aim of this procedure is to provide more detailed information about the interests identified in step two (information that will be useful in determining the fairness of a settlement).

In so far as identification of utilitarian gains for the other party (either worker or client) encourages both parties to view the issue from the other's perspective, it is especially useful in helping them to recognise that some of their demands may be unfair. Ultimately, however, there can be no guarantee that worker and client will employ the same standards in assessing fairness, so where the decisional balance sheet approach fails to produce a satisfactory result, it can be useful to call in an objective third party (if one can be found) to go through the decisional balance grids and arbitrate a settlement.

*Step six: agree on methods for monitoring progress*

Although it might seem obvious that worker and client should agree on what they will accept as sufficient progress to justify renegotiating and perhaps even terminating their relationship, it is surprising how frequently this step is overlooked. Conversely, until there is a crisis it is common for workers to ignore the issue of what should be done if the client breaches one of the terms of the agreement. Such oversights on the social worker's part make it likely that the worker will resort to unilateral action when and if casework gets into trouble. Inevitably, the end result of such action will be bitterness on the client's part; he or she rightly sees it as a denial of all the principles of negotiation which had been professed up to now.

It is essential, therefore, that a negotiated casework plan incorporate specific criteria for monitoring progress. Before intervention begins, worker and client should discuss each aspect of the case plan and decide on how the plan can be monitored. How will we know that intervention is working? What should happen if the client fails to comply with one or more of the terms? Precisely what is required before social work intervention can be terminated or renegotiated? Such questions are asked at this point and detailed, behaviourally-specific replies must be sought. It is insufficient, for example, to propose to parents that their child protection plan can be renegotiated when there is improvement in the client's level of parenting skills. Such a criterion begs basic questions about what constitutes improvement, how much improvement is required, and how improvement will be assessed.

The steps outlined in this chapter are designed both to maximise client power in the involuntary casework relationship and to satisfy as many of the client's legitimate interests as possible. However, as pointed out previously, the very concept of negotiation presupposes that not all client interests can be met fully. For the client as well as the worker, concessions are inevitable. In step five we looked at the need to assess fairness in negotiated settlements, but where it is not possible to attain a result which is satisfactory to the client, the worker may resort to bargaining to prevent negotiations from breaking down entirely. For example, the probation officer might compensate the probationer for visiting the agency (rather than the worker having to pay a home visit) by agreeing to minimise contact visits or to work on another problem which the client is keen to resolve. However, despite the worker's best efforts, there will always be some clients who steadfastly refuse to work towards a negotiated settlement. Such individuals cannot get past their hostility at having to submit to social work intervention and will simply restate their opposition despite whatever efforts are made to direct attention to the interests underlying their hostility. In such cases, the worker him- or herself can embark on steps three to six in the presence of the client but without the benefit of the client's input. Thus, with the client sitting through the process, the worker can identify all the non-negotiable and negotiable aspects of social work intervention, construct the case plan and decide on procedures for monitoring progress. More often than not, the process of thinking aloud through these steps will be enough to entice the client into negotiating. But where even this tactic fails to engage the client, at least the worker will have demonstrated a willingness to negotiate and a desire to take account of the client's right to influence the terms of the relationship.

# 5

# Community Work Theory

A claim which is continually repeated in the community work literature is that practice theory remains disjointed and underdeveloped (Schwartz, 1977; Kramer and Specht, 1983; J. Fisher, 1984; S.H. Taylor and Roberts, 1985; Rothman and Tropman, 1987). There is even a tendency for some authors (such as York, 1984) to look longingly at the casework literature which they believe is better able than community work theory to guide the actions of its practitioners. But while the community work literature may be disjointed, it is hard to see why it should be described as underdeveloped. At least since the decolonisation activities of European powers earlier this century, a plethora of practice approaches have found their way into the community work literature. The real problems for practitioners relate more to the classification and choice of theories rather than to the dearth of them.

In an effort to put some order into the chaos, different authors have presented different community work typologies over the years. An early taxonomy was that of Ross (1958), who distinguished between three substantive orientations in working with communities: (a) reformist, (b) planning, and (c) process or community development approaches. A decade or so later, the so-called Gulbenkian Study Group (1968) identified three 'aspects' of community work which it said accounted for most of the extant literature: (a) direct community development work with sub-groups of the population, (b) methods for facilitating agency and inter-agency coordination, and (c) methods of social planning and policy formulation. York (1984) rejects the notion that community work theories can be categorised into neatly distinct types like this, and prefers to think in terms of continua on which all approaches can be lined up. According to him, the most meaningful continuum is directiveness, with community work models coming in somewhere between the 'totally directive' and 'totally non-directive' poles. In a similar way, Gilbert and Specht (1977) locate community work models on a task versus process continuum, while Grosser (1973) employs a similar distinction to York with his 'initiating' versus 'enabling' continuum.

By far the most celebrated taxonomy of community work theories, however, is Rothman's (1979) 'three models' formulation. Based on earlier work by Ross (1958) and by Morris and Binstock (1966), Rothman distinguished between locality development, social planning and social action approaches to community work, and compared them all in terms of eleven practice dimensions including, for example, basic change strategy, practitioner roles, orientation towards power structures and client roles. According to Rothman, locality development approaches aim at community change through the broadest possible participation of local community members. Among other things, these approaches emphasise democratic procedures, voluntary cooperation, self-help, and the development of indigenous leadership (see also Dunham, 1963). Social planning approaches, on the other hand, concentrate on the technical processes of problem-solving in regard to specific social problems such as unemployment, housing or health. Finally, social action approaches are said to encompass methods directed at redistributing power, resources or decision-making away from more powerful and towards less powerful sections of the community.

In this chapter we shall distinguish between community work approaches according to whether they emphasise consensus or conflict. The approaches roughly correspond to Rothman's locality development and social action models but, by focusing more on the mechanisms responsible for change, the implications for practice and the decisions facing the worker in the third phase of our model become more apparent.

**Consensus models**

Much of the inspiration for consensus approaches to community work has come from the community development activities of colonial powers (particularly Britain), which aimed at helping the native populations cope with rapid social and political changes occurring inside and outside the colonies from around the turn of the century. The Battens (Batten 1965a, 1965b; Batten and Batten, 1967), two of the chief architects of this tradition, wrote from a background of community work in African villages under the British Development and Welfare Acts which sought to arrest the disintegration of village communities and the consequent drift towards townships. Their work was conducted in close-knit communities often of less than 100 individuals, where unity of purpose and social harmony could almost be assumed. Not surprisingly, the Battens could conceive of community work interventions which were successful for *all* members of the community. Indeed, according to them, a community worker had to raise the general level of satisfaction within the community; an objective which involved 'tension reduction' and the avoidance of social turmoil or disintegration. According to Batten (1965a), community development is a threefold process. First, people are stimulated to decide what change(s) they want in their local community. The task of the worker at this stage is to help the community pinpoint any 'dissatisfactions' they might have and give community members faith in their ability to help themselves. The second process is educational and involves the worker in proposing possible solutions to the community's dissatisfactions. The third process involves maintaining existing community groups or developing new ones to ensure that all individuals have opportunities for developing their personalities and achieving status and significance within the community. The Battens' main vehicle for accomplishing these tasks was local discussion groups, which generate ideas and involve participants in communal problem-solving efforts.

In a similar spirit to the Battens, Ross (1955, 1958), Ross and Lappin (1967) and William and Loureide Biddle (Biddle and Biddle, 1965) began developing models for non-directive community work which would try to resolve community problems through cooperation and participation in decision-making. In an oft-quoted passage, Ross and Lappin (1967) define community development as:

> a process by which a community identifies its needs or objectives, orders (or ranks) these needs or objectives, develops the confidence and will to work at these needs or objectives, takes action in respect to them, and in so doing extends and develops cooperative and collaborative attitudes and practices in the community. (p. 39)

As with the Battens, Ross and Lappin place considerable emphasis on developing the community's capacity to function as an integrated unit through involvement with the community on one or more local problems. Writing from within a Western industrialised country, Ross and Lappin naturally recognised that there would be sectional interests within a community so they stressed that the identification of community needs must take account of all sub-groupings. The authors assume that as the problem-solving process unfolds, sub-groups will come to understand, accept and work with other sub-groups and develop skills in overcoming conflict. To this end, the community worker aims to increase community members' identification with the community as a whole, as well as their interest and participation in the community. From Ross and Lappin's perspective, then, community work involves two essential processes: (a) planning, and (b) community integration.

Ross and Lappin (1967) set out five basic roles for the community worker. The first and most important of them is that of guide. As guide, the community worker helps the community establish its priorities and find its means for goal attainment. The authors insist that decisions be left to the community even when the worker knows that a certain decision is likely to produce harmful effects. In this Ross and Lappin compare the community worker to a psychiatrist who remains neutral and non-judgemental at all times: '[The community worker] tries not to be part of a "left wing" or "right wing", of a higher or lower class, with advocates of socialised medicine or advocates of private enterprise in the health field' (p. 211). As well as guide, the community worker acts in the role of enabler. He or she tries to focus community dissatisfactions, to encourage community organisation, to nourish good interpersonal relations within the community and to emphasise common objectives. At a lower level of priority, the community worker functions in the role of expert; but Ross and Lappin stress that the worker's expertise must be confined to providing 'facts' and 're-sources', not directions. For example, the worker can provide information about other communities or, advice on methods of organisation and procedure, as well as technical information about such matters as the political processes involved in policy formulation. Finally, the community worker functions as a social therapist. The authors draw a rather odd parallel between the work of psychiatrists with individuals and the actions of community workers with entire communities. Community workers seek to 'diagnose' and 'treat' the community by helping key community members to recognise and modify the underlying forces which divide various groups of the community.

The notion of 'enabling' is very strong within this change-by-consensus tradition in community work (cf. Lappin, 1985). The term was apparently introduced to distinguish community development from community organising of the kind discussed below (Dunham, 1959). In one of the first papers to use the term, Newstetter (1947) developed a model of community enabling composed of 43 enabling functions grouped into seven categories of practice skill. The practice skills were grouped in turn into three basic enabling roles that were said to be characteristic of community development work: (a) promoting the development of community structures for the purpose of problem resolution; (b) helping individuals in the community to function as community representatives; and (c) helping community sub-groups to collaborate with other sub-groups.

More recent change-by-consensus models have been developed by Henderson and Thomas (1980), and by Bedics and Doelker (1983). Henderson and Thomas's is a process model of locality development which contains nine stages of 'neighbourhood work', and each of the stages provides detailed prescriptions for practice. The nine stages are:

1. planning and negotiating entry (to the neighbourhood);
2. getting to know the community;
3. working out what to do next;
4. making contacts and bringing people together;
5. forming and building organizations;
6. helping to clarify goals and priorities;
7. keeping the organization going;
8. dealing with friends and enemies;
9. leavings and endings.

Throughout the process there is implicit acceptance of the kind of enabling function which is the hallmark of all change-by-consensus approaches. Rothman and Tropman's (1987) description of this kind of function is such a good summary of change-by-consensus approaches that it is worth quoting them at some length:

> [In these approaches] goals of action include self-help and increased community capacity and integration. The community, especially in urban contexts, is seen as eclipsed, fragmented, suffering from anomie, and with a lack of good human relationships and democratic problem-solving skills. The basic change strategy involves getting a broad cross section of people involved in studying and taking action on their problems. Consensus strategies are employed, involving small-group discussion and fostering communication among community subparts (class, ethnic, and so forth). The practitioner functions as an enabler and catalyst as well as a teacher of problem-solving skills and ethical values. He/she is especially skilled in manipulating and guiding small-group interaction. Members of power structures are collaborators in a common effort since the definition of the community client system includes the total geographic community. The practitioner conceives of the community as composed of common interests or reconcilable differences. Clients are conceived of as citizens engaged in a common community venture,

and their role accordingly is one of participating in an
interactional problem-solving process. (p. 17)

It is common for community work to be seen by practitioners as inherently progressive because of its focus on
people's expressed needs and its participation in clients' lives
at a 'grass roots' level. Accordingly, there is a tendency to
prefix social work programmes at every available opportunity with the adjective 'community'. This somehow makes
them sound more 'relevant', even radical, to the ears of jaded
workers and their clients. Indeed, Jones (1977) once described community as an 'aerosol word' because of the
hopeful way it gets 'sprayed over deteriorating (welfare)
institutions' (p. 26) to make them more contemporary and
relevant to society's ills. Even the laudable Griffiths Report
(1988), and a great deal of the discussion surrounding it (cf.
Cohen 1989; Cohen and Eaton, 1989; Fawcett, 1989;
Heptinsall, 1989; Leigh, 1989), have been liberally sprayed
with terms like '*community* care', '*community* participation'
and '*community* self-determination', as if the nature of the
descriptor was both self-evident and, like motherhood,
entirely above dissension. But the fact is that there is
nothing self-evident or intrinsically progressive about 'community work', and social workers who seek to operationalise
the Griffiths recommendations by relying exclusively on the
kind of change-by-consensus tradition reviewed above are
unlikely to alter the fundamental circumstances of their
clients' lives beyond facilitating a shift in the focus of care
from one place (the institution) to another (the community).

The reason for this ideological conservatism concerns the
consensus view of the way communities should work. As
Rothman and Tropman (1987) make clear, the notion of
community implicit in locality development is a romantic,
social system characterised by cooperation and harmony.
Plant (1974) has traced the roots of this community work
tradition to pre-industrial Europe where the existence of
oppression, intolerance and persecution have been overlooked by community work in its infatuation with the
seemingly idyllic, uncomplicated existence of village life. In
short, change-by-consensus models dream of resuscitating

the social relations of a bygone era. Ross and Lappin's (1967) fatuous image of the community worker as a kind of barefoot psychotherapist may be one of the more graphic illustrations of this sentimental quest for communal reconciliation and harmony, but their basic assumptions concerning 'community' are shared by other locality development writers. Problems in contemporary society's attainment of 'community' are attributed to modernisation rather than to class and oppressive political structures. Thus, protagonists of locality development conceive of the rediscovery of community as a *technical* rather than a *political* problem. As Khinduka (1987) puts it:

> The besetting limitation of community development as a strategy for social change is its psychological rather than socioeconomic approach to social problems. Community development programs aim at revolutionary change in the people's psychology without bringing about an actual revolution in their socioeconomic relations. They are concerned with people's psychological capacity to make decisions, not with their economic power to do so. (p. 358)

These flawed assumptions of locality or community development find expression in practice methods which are politically non-partisan and which emphasise conflict resolution. To these characteristics we can almost always add a tendency on the part of most writers to think of 'community' solely in territorial terms. Taken together these are the aspects of community work practice which make the models outlined so far an inadequate base from which to launch the social action component of our own approach to practice. A social worker who comes to community organisation from a background of casework with marginalised groups is almost *certain* to be partisan, and he or she requires methods which are capable of advancing the sectional interests of clients. For this reason, the attempt by locality developers to extend an impartial counselling mentality to community work is most unhelpful. Under our model, community workers may not have a clear vision of all the details but the direction and beneficiaries of change will be pre-set by the time the worker arrives at the community organisation phase of our model.

Related to the issue of partisanship is the need for methods which embrace conflict. It is simply not possible to extend the analysis of small, pre-industrial territorial units to modern urban society, and a community worker cannot conduct an accurate community analysis without awareness of the distribution of power and the forces opposed to change within and without that community. To put this another way, Western capitalism is not built on consensus but on conflict, and if community work is to improve the lot of marginalised groups we require practice methods which are instructive in the *use* of conflict, not its resolution.

Finally, from our viewpoint, the notion of community need not normally correspond to a territorial unit at all but to representatives of an oppressed class or sub-group. It may be that the individuals with whom we work do reside in close geographical proximity, but this is not essential to our model. Indeed, even if we are forced by the terms of our employment to confine our activities to certain geographical boundaries, social workers in the later stages of our model will normally be seeking to advance the interests of only a section of that community. Under these circumstances models which emphasise the need to engage the entire geographical community in solving the problem are likely to act against the interests of our client group.

All of this does not mean that locality development models do not have their place, and neither does it mean they have nothing whatever to offer us. They may be insufficient for our purposes, but they are not useless. In the chapter which follows the reader will detect an emphasis on promoting group cohesion and democratic decision-making within the client group itself and the change-by-consensus tradition is strong on this point. Collaboration, group reflection and non-directiveness are all tactics which must be employed by the worker in his or her dealings with a fledgeling client group. If the group is to become an effective lobby group it must achieve internal harmony and unity of purpose, and one of the worker's two main tasks during the transition phase of our model is to promote this kind of group development. However, as the intervention gathers momentum and the group begins to look outward during the community organisation phase, change-by-consensus strategies are of little practical value.

## Conflict approaches

By contrast to the consensus or locality development models reviewed above, community work methods that advocate the strategic use of conflict make no effort to work towards universally acceptable solutions. Community workers who operate from a conflict perspective seek only to advance the sectional interests of their particular client group. It is assumed that political conflict is an inherent feature of society and for one section of society to benefit from change, another section must be disadvantaged (cf. R. Fisher, 1987). More than this, conflict approaches contend that structural inequality, and not individual deficiency, is ultimately responsible for the privations of the poor. Political participation in the conventional pluralistic channels of society is said not to include the full spectrum of citizens.

Conflict approaches aim to build a grass roots coalition of citizens. The organisation may grow up around a single issue such as creating a needed service, or it may embrace a broader social agenda involving the transfer of power away from decision-making elites towards the grass roots coalition itself. Often in the former case and always in the latter case the actions of the organisation will be contentious and bitterly resisted. Grosser and Mondros (1985) see three basic roles for the worker engaged in this kind of community work. First is the role of educator wherein the worker encourages members of the client organisation to reflect on their circumstances, partialise their problems and speculate about possible solutions. In effect, the worker politicises group members by helping them make the intellectual connection between their personal problems and underlying sociopolitical structures. As we shall see, much of the inspiration for this role derives from Paulo Freire's (1972a, 1972b) ideas concerning 'conscientisation' of the poor. As well as developing group members' political understanding, the educational role of conflict-oriented community workers extends to collaborating with group members to build the people's organisation, to help design workable meeting procedures and to facilitate the execution of other administrative tasks. The second role referred to by Grosser and Mondros is that of resource developer. This role involves research of the kind we will discuss in the next chapter, as well as fund-raising, acquiring staff and meeting facilities, helping with press releases, and so on. Finally, the worker facilitates political action. He or she 'rubs raw the sores of discontent' (Grosser and Mondros, 1985, p. 162) in an effort to inflame community discontent and heighten members' resolve to win.

Among the best known and most clearly articulated conflict models of practice are those developed by Saul Alinsky (1969, 1971) and the neo-Alinskyists (J. Fisher, 1984; Kahn, 1970, 1982). Under the Alinsky method, community workers must be highly trained catalysts of social change. Far from the non-directive social therapist role envisaged by Ross and Lappin (1967), Alinsky's ideal community organiser leads from the front. Despite constant references to the sovereignty of the community group, Alinsky's strategy nevertheless placed great emphasis on the need for a professional organiser: one who is capable of mobilising and guiding community opinion, interpreting events and facilitating negotiations with authorities. Of greatest importance is the worker's task of building a 'People's Organisation' (Haggstrom, 1987). The People's Organisation is a democratic, community-based group representing the community, and it should gradually take over more and more of the leadership until the worker is out of a job completely. Although the People's Organisation is formed around a single issue or set of related issues, Alinsky intended that the association extend beyond the initial problem and become a mediating structure between decision-makers and the community.

Power and conflict are key concepts within the Alinsky tradition. Alinsky believed that the mere existence of democratic structures in society did not guarantee that everyone's voice would be heard. Only by organising people to fight for power can true democracy be recognised. Alinsky scorned traditional consensus approaches to community work and argued that people without money or political influence could only achieve power by using militant tactics. The more disturbing the tactic to those in power, the better. Alinsky (1969) once wrote:

> A People's Organization is a conflict group... Its sole reason for coming into being is to wage war... Because the character of a People's Organization is such that it will frequently involve itself in conflict, and since most attempts at the building of People's Organizations have been broken by the attacks of an opposition which knows no rules of fair play or so-called ethics, it is imperative that the organisers and leaders of a People's Organization not only understand the necessity for and the nature and purpose of conflict tactics, but become familiar with and skilful in the use of such tactics. (p. 132–3)

Alinskyism is not above anything: riots, strikes, blackmail or anything else that might force the enemy to negotiate, all are legitimate weapons of war. Alinsky also exhorted People's Organisations to be 'practical' and unfettered by 'ideology'. His reasons for doing so were twofold. In the first place, he believed that ideological organisations are intrinsically undemocratic because their leaders have preconceived ideas about the ultimate purpose of the organisation. Alinsky's view was that the neighbourhood should be left to decide, no matter what they decided. It was not necessary that their decisions be consistent with a broader vision or programme of social change. In the second place, ideology constrains action and, as we have already seen, Alinsky's view was that the end justifies any means. Ideological proscriptions must not be allowed to stand in the way. The irony of Alinsky's 'pragmatism', of course, is that it is implicitly grounded in the ideology of pluralism. He believed that 'the system' could work for the poor if only they could get to the bargaining table and take up a position of strength there. In other words, the Alinsky approach accepts an interest-group model of democracy in which various groups compete for resources. Alinsky offers no critique of the political and economic system whatever, no analysis (other than powerlessness) of the causes of poverty, and no solution to social problems beyond acquiring power.

Neo-Alinskyists recognise that the poor need more than power: they also need political education (cf. J. Fisher, 1984). They need an analysis which addresses issues of class, race, gender and democratic values, not just tactics and power. The aim is not to indoctrinate the poor but to provide them with opportunities for discussion and a perspective on their plight which clarifies the role of underlying social structures. Neo-Alinskyism differs from the Alinsky approach in at least two other important ways. First, neo-Alinskyists seek to develop *mass* political organisations that, although rooted in local concerns, nevertheless go beyond the local unit. The Alinsky-style organising of the 1960s limited itself to a particular neighbourhood or ethnic group and so could be accused of pitting one oppressed group against another. For their part, Neo-Alinskyists look for opportunities to connect up grassroots organisations into a larger political force. Second, neo-Alinskyists repudiate the professionalism of Alinsky's method. They reject Alinsky's emphasis on professionally trained organisers and place a greater value on identifying and encouraging local leadership.

The neo-Alinskyist organisation 'Association of Community Organisations for Reform Now' (ACORN), developed a programme of community organisation which can be summarised in six points. The first point is the injunction 'The people shall rule', which is meant to serve as a reminder to the worker that he or she must start with local concerns and not go in with preconceived ideas about what the community needs to do. The second point is to develop community contacts by getting people's names and talking with them in their homes where possible. Third, organise a house meeting of less than a dozen people. This small group will be the foundation of a larger People's Organisation so it should be representative of the community. As well as discussing personal concerns, the group should begin to identify common concerns and issues, thereby promoting group solidarity and heightening people's determination to struggle. Fourth, promote the group by looking for and including other like-minded individuals in the group. Fifth, identify an issue which is likely to galvanise the community. More important than the issue itself is its capacity to get people involved in the organisation. Sixth, hold a major public meeting to discuss the issue. This meeting will formalise the organisation and launch it on a programme of social action. Local organisations formed in this way then become part of a larger coalition which promotes cooperation and looks for common ground.

Except for its definition of 'community' as being a coalition of clients united by a common problem or set of problems rather than a neighbourhood unit, the approach to community work outlined in Chapters 6 and 7 comes very close to the ACORN model. As we shall see, the process of community organising gathers momentum from small group discussion through to formal organisation in a similar way and for identical reasons as ACORN's neo-Alinskyist approach.

Conflict approaches based more on the work of Paulo Freire than Saul Alinsky were also experimented with by workers employed in the British Community Development Projects (CDPs) during the early 1970s. These projects were launched in 1969 throughout Britain as one of a series of initiatives to attack urban poverty. Like the American War on Poverty, the CDPs were founded on the assumption that poverty is due to inadequacies within poor communities: that is, to their inability to compete for a share of the national wealth. The CDPs further assumed that opportunities for overcoming poverty did exist and that what was needed was to help the poor take advantage of the opportunities offered them. Accordingly, a key element of the CDPs was education in the use of local social services, and to this end certain educational priority areas were identified. The programmes were aimed particularly at ethnic minorities, especially immigrants from the West Indies and the Indian subcontinent who were concentrated in the unskilled workforce.

In practice, the CDPs developed a much more radical orientation than the British Home Office ever intended. Many CDP workers moved away from the localist orientation of the programme towards a view of poverty as being due to broader structural injustice. Despite being employed as community development workers Ashcroft and Jackson (1974), for example, concluded that community development does nothing for the poor because it ignores the fact that poverty results from a social system which is based on exploitation. Many CDP workers, including Ashcroft and Jackson, were openly critical of the programme's obsession with 'locally relevant' education because it limited the horizons of the poor, stood in the way of class consciousness and ignored the 'locally irrelevant' forces that were creating deprivation in the first place. Ashcroft and Jackson argued for education which is relevant not just to the individual but also to the class of which the individual is a member. They rejected the whole notion of education for self-advancement in favour of educating for class solidarity. Their educational strategy consisted of explaining to the poor that their needs do not arise from living in poor communities but from their membership of the working class. In one of their attempts to achieve this, Ashcroft and Jackson held a one-day conference on certain provisions of the Housing Finance Act which they endeavoured to show discriminated against the poor. A public meeting followed at which a lobby group was formed. Under Ashcroft and Jackson's guidance, the group used their experiences and examination of the Act to study the ways in which the political system successfully marginalised them. This emphasis on guided, small group reflection is strongly reminiscent of Freire's (1970, 1972a and b) 'pedagogy of the oppressed' and introduces an aspect of community work which is under-valued in the Alinsky and neo-Alinsky approaches.

In the chapters which follow we will attempt to operationalise an approach to social work practice that is largely founded on the conflict tradition in community organisation. While a number of the strategies may be reminiscent of neo-Alinskyism, ours is an approach which also seeks to accommodate Freire's (1970, 1972a and b) concern for education through collective reflection.

Like Alinsky and the neo-Alinskyists, the formation of a politically competent People's Organisation is crucial to our community organisation method. Not only is the People's

Organisation the vehicle for advancing the interests of our client group, it is also a powerful influence on the participants themselves. The People's Organisation helps free participants from learned helplessness, the psychological legacy of oppression. It opens their eyes to the structural obstacles confronting them, and it educates them in the political processes governing their lives. These intellectual and psychological advances are achieved not through the formal education system or the provision of remedial services like those first envisaged by the CDPs, but through involvement in the struggle for social change. Also like Alinsky, the steps outlined in the remainder of the book are largely reformist. The agenda that is set out makes no claim to being 'radical' in the sense of attacking the fundamental structures supporting injustice. Rather, the process seeks tangible concessions for our clients in the short term. Of course there is nothing in our approach to stop workers and clients moving on from demands for reform to more radical objectives, and this issue is canvassed in the final chapter. The present model also accepts the need for leadership on the part of the community organiser. The model rejects the sterile image of a non-directive counsellor handing out empathy to marginalised community groups. Our model accepts that the ultimate aim of community organising is to promote client self-determination but, in order to achieve this goal, the worker must be prepared to act as motivator and mentor to the People's Organisation for as long as it takes for them to acquire the skills to carry on alone. The reader will also recognise another standard Alinskyist strategy: that of looking for immediate, direct threats to the client group's self-interest around which to galvanise group members.

Unlike Alinsky, our model does not advocate resorting to *any* tactic that is capable of bringing 'the enemy' to the negotiating table. Our procedures seek to provide the worker with strategies for planning tactics, but most of the examples given exert pressure on decision-makers rather than bludgeon them into submission. In the end, decisions about how far workers and clients are prepared to go in mounting their campaign will depend on their own value systems and the reader is left to decide this issue for him- or herself. A further difference between our approach and Alinsky's is that our model advocates starting slowly, with small mutual-support groups. As we shall see, the aim of this strategy is twofold: first, it is necessary to build solidarity before embarking on any campaign of social action; and second, it provides a setting for engaging in the kind of group reflection advocated by Freire (1970, 1972a and b).

This brief overview of consensus and conflict approaches to community work provides a theoretical framework for the remainder of the book. As our model moves away from primarily casework interventions through the formation of small, unstructured client groups to the incorporation of client organisations, we will draw on this literature to guide our actions. Though the following two chapters deal with the 'nuts and bolts' of moving from casework to community organisation, much of the rationale for these activities has now been covered. The transition phase of our model deals with the worker's efforts to bring clients together in a supportive and non-directive forum to discuss and reflect on mutual problems. Both through this process and through involvement in the struggle for social reform, the clients' political education should be advanced. The community organisation phase then takes up the Alinsky and neo-Alinsky challenge of building a People's Organisation and seeks to describe some of the more important steps in launching a campaign of social action. As previously noted, the final chapter considers the relationship between the reformist goals of community organising and the promotion of a more radical social agenda.

# 6

# The Transition to Political Activity

In Chapter 1 it was argued that the social worker who approaches human problems from a truly holistic perspective will eventually become aware of the need for policy reform. This transition from lower system level activity to political insight can take the accumulated experience of many unsuccessful or inadequately-resolved case plans. As case-workers endeavour to resolve problems on a case-by-case basis, they will come to recognise certain patterns or regularities in their clients' circumstances that act to perpetuate their problems: for example, child protection workers may recognise a close association between child abuse, unemployment and social isolation. Similarly, psychiatric social workers are likely to discover that their clients' inability to cope in the community is related to a lack of opportunity and inadequate community-based services. When insights such as these have been achieved, the case-worker enters the 'transition phase' of our model, for it is at this point that the worker begins to move towards interventions which involve political activity. Intervention now takes two vitally important directions. First, individual clients must be brought together to break down the isolation which ultimately contributes to their powerlessness; the worker will try to instil a sense of solidarity in the group and encourage group reflection on the problems being experienced by group members. Second, work must begin on accumulating evidence capable of attracting public sympathy and pressuring social policy-makers during the community organisation phase that will follow.

## Bringing clients together

A latent cost of casework practice is isolation. As long as clients are dealt with on a case-by-case basis, they are denied the opportunity of seeing themselves as members of an oppressed *class* rather than merely individuals in trouble. For this reason, making the transition from individual client to group member is undoubtedly the most crucial point in the present model of practice. One of the enduring themes of the social work literature has been that social work seeks to optimise the client's capacity for self-determination and this ideal is obviously inconsistent with working only *for* clients. As Freire (1971a, 1972b) continually pointed out, a policy of working *for* the poor is ultimately destructive, reinforcing 'the culture of silence' that oppresses them and confirming their view of themselves as subordinate and dependent. A similar point has also been made by Scott (1981) in defence of his proposal that more 'voluntary' or non-government agencies should expand their role to include social activism. According to Scott, the voluntary organisation can provide the poor with a 'mediating structure' which collectivises their concerns and enables them to speak with confidence to social policy-makers. In his book, Scott is particularly critical of social workers whom he accuses of being afraid of conflict and preoccupied with non-directiveness, traits which he holds responsible for social work's poor record in social action. According to Scott, the solution is for non-government welfare organisations to broaden their focus from remedial work to social activism and to create opportunities for engaging clients in the social change efforts of the agency.

The potential of client-based organisations to influence participants has been demonstrated by Kieffer (1987), whose systematic study of individuals who emerged from oppressed communities provides an insight into the process by which the poor are moved into action. Kieffer was interested in how oppressed minorities can achieve a sense of what he called 'participatory competence', or political activism born of the conviction that social conditions can change if the poor are organised and assertive. Kieffer's study identified four distinct stages in the movement to participatory competence. In the first stage, 'the era of entry', the soon-to-be political figure was confronted with a tangible, direct threat to his or her individual self-interest. There is considerable agreement in the community work literature (see Dunham, 1970; Baldock, 1974; Brager and Specht, 1973; Henderson and Thomas, 1980; Twelvetrees, 1982) that long-term oppression is more likely to be tolerated than is a sudden setback or threat to one's self-interest, even if that threat is trivial by comparison with the more fundamental privations of one's life. According to Kieffer, this occurrence is followed by a period during which political participation is explored in a clumsy and unknowing fashion. This is a period of self-discovery, of coming to know one's capacity for impact and of de-mystifying power and status. Importantly, Kieffer found that there was a crucial prerequisite before the era of entry (into the political process) could begin. He labelled this prerequisite 'integrity', by which he meant feelings of pride and determination, and of rootedness within a supportive and caring community. Thus integrity and the community which spawns it provide a secure base from which the political process can be explored.

Kieffer's findings concerning the 'era of entry' help clarify the caseworker's primary role during this phase of our model. By bringing clients together in a mutually supportive forum, the worker helps to create the sense of integrity which is a prerequisite to collective action. In the early stages of the group's life, therefore, political activity takes second place to the goal of promoting group cohesion. Assuming clients agree to come together because they share some common problem or need, creating opportunities for participants to discuss their circumstances with others should promote this sense of empathy and belonging of which Kieffer speaks. To begin with, group members will naturally look to the worker to provide leadership and structure in the meetings and, if the worker resists this expectation, participants will feel threatened and confused by their lack of direction. As a result some, maybe even most, will stop attending. To avoid this, the worker should come to the first few meetings with a clear agenda in mind (if not on paper) and be prepared to guide the meeting through its business. It can be helpful to divide these early meetings into three roughly equal parts. First, the worker can provide structured input in the form of a guest speaker or videotape so that group members can ease into the meeting without feeling under pressure to speak up or perform in any way. Next, the worker could try to promote discussion (not just questions) around the issues raised during the presentation. Finally, when the formal part of the meeting is concluded, members should be invited to have a cup of tea and socialise for a while. The whole process should take less than two hours and group members must be informed at the outset of the meeting precisely what the activities are to be.

It is during the second part of the meeting – the discussion stage – that the vital issue of leadership will begin to emerge, provided of course that the worker him- or herself does not dominate the conversation. The group will come to expect certain members to stimulate discussion and make suggestions, others might tend to ask questions, while others might be good at summarising and clarifying things. Within a few weeks of this kind of semi-structured discussion, group members will start to feel relaxed in the group because they will have taken up a role in that group with which they and others feel comfortable. Any participants who do not find a comfortable role in discussion will drop out.

Notwithstanding the absolute necessity of allowing group members themselves to take the discussion wherever they choose, the worker nevertheless looks for opportunities to make salient any immediate policy issue that threatens the interests of the group. The threat that is identified must relate to the underlying pattern in clients' circumstances that was identified by the worker during the casework phase of our model. It may be the imminent closure of a child-care centre, or the failure of the local council to provide a much-needed service in the area, or any other direct, tangible affront to the group's interests. Such issues provide an ideal springboard to political action. In line with the principles outlined in Chapter 3, problems that are identified at this early stage should be relatively minor and capable of being influenced by a politically inexperienced group. At this point in the group's life, the issue itself is not nearly as important as the process of working together towards its resolution.

As group discussion continues over the weeks, group members themselves will begin to contribute ideas for addressing common issues or problems. Early suggestions are normally politically naive activities, such as taking up a petition or writing to a government minister. Nevertheless, suggestions like this represent a crucial turning point in the life of the group. In the first place, the focus of leadership will begin to move away from the worker towards an individual or individuals in the group who are prepared to take the front running on the project. In addition, group meetings will now tend to revolve around the project, thereby relieving the worker of the need to organise and structure all meetings. Finally, early projects provide the point of entry into what is likely to become an escalating campaign of political action. For example, after the petition has been taken up, it will have to be followed up and, if the group is fobbed off or treated condescendingly by government bureaucrats, it will have to find some other, more persuasive, means of delivering its message.

Thus, provided that the early meetings are negotiated successfully and the group stays together, the work will move towards social action. As Kieffer (1984) found, after the era of entry there comes an 'era of advancement' during which group members, through engagement in the political arena, become aware of the interconnections between social, political and economic relations. Gradually the group will become immersed in the kind of campaign activities described in the next chapter. As a result of their experiences, great advances can be expected in group members' critical understanding of society and especially of the role of powerful vested interests in the construction of social policy. This intellectual breakthrough is the political education spoken of in the previous chapter and it provides the motivation for social action. Over time, group members will come to understand why things are as they are and how they could be different. As in Kieffer's (1984) first 'era', supportive peer relationships remain an essential ingredient at this stage, as is the active support of a mentor who is more experienced in political processes. Thus, although the worker tries to identify and encourage group leaders during the transition to community organising, he or she must also be prepared to remain on hand to elucidate the complex political processes involved in mounting a campaign, no matter how limited in scope.

The third stage in the development of participatory competence is referred to by Kieffer (1984) as 'the era of incorporation', during which individuals can be expected to confront and learn to contend with the permanence of structural barriers to self-determination. While their experience of political participation during the earlier stage may make group members aware of the limits of collective action, this stage should see them incorporate into their self-image an altered perception of themselves as politically competent and involved. Finally, during the 'era of commitment', participants can be expected to search for viable ways of applying their new-found abilities and insights by committing themselves to a career or line of action that provides an outlet for the personal and political advances which have been achieved through political participation.

Community groups embarking on a programme of social reform must expect to meet with stiff resistance at some point in their activities. In anticipation of this resistance, transition work must also involve preparing a persuasive case in favour of reform. Armed with evidence of the need for reform, the group can go forward into the public arena with confidence. The worker has a vital role to play in formulating this case. As we shall see, the worker has access to certain kinds of data that can be invaluable in supporting a campaign. While the group is in its formative stages and engrossed in planning its activities, the worker begins to collect this information and feed it into group meetings. It is to the fair and foul means of gathering campaign evidence that we now turn.

## Gathering the evidence

Although providing evidence of the need for change necessitates the use of standardised methods of need assessment, it will become obvious to the reader that the activity proposed during this transition phase is far from objective or scientific.

The intention is to prove rather than assess need. This is not to say that the worker enters the transition phase with an entirely closed mind; there will be much about the situation which is unknown but which must be understood before the clients' situation can be improved. What precisely needs to change and how can it best be accomplished? What do the clients themselves want? If some new service is necessary, how should it be funded, delivered and managed? Questions such as these will often be addressed during the transition phase. Nevertheless, there is (at the very least) a presumption that change *is* necessary and that clients must be the major beneficiaries. For this reason, the caseworker goes about the task more as a lawyer preparing an argument than an objective researcher interested only in facts. In other words, 'need assessment' during the transition phase is a political rather than a scientific exercise and the caseworker gathers whatever data are available to support the forthcoming campaign. In this section we will consider three broad approaches to data collection: (a) the social indicator approach, (b) survey approaches, and (c) community group approaches. Both from a political and a scientific vantage point, the best data collection strategies normally combine elements of all three.

*Social indicators*

By definition, an indicator is an indirect measure of the phenomenon under investigation; it suggests the presence of some reality rather than measuring it directly. Social indicators are thus particularly useful when the variable of interest is somehow elusive or unmeasurable. For example, the investigator may appeal to figures on the cost of vandalism within a community to make claims about the level of alienation within that community. Clearly, vandalism is not the same thing as alienation but the researcher draws an inference about the level of one from the level of the other. Decisions about which specific indicators to select are determined by pragmatic as well as logical considerations. The worker will need to establish what data bases are readily available and what information can be extracted to support the need for reform. There are normally several primary sources of social indicators. Census data is perhaps the most obvious and accessible of these sources. Not only are the reports prepared by government census departments an invaluable source in themselves, but those same departments are normally able to provide statistical information about regions nominated by the researcher. Thus the worker can, for example, make comparisons between the general community and a particular region of interest. As well as census collection departments, local councils keep detailed information on housing characteristics, income, and other economic and social data relevant to their constituency. Similarly, government health and welfare departments keep epidemiological and incidence data from which inferences can be drawn.

One of the most powerful and accessible (yet frequently overlooked) sources of indicators, however, is the caseworker's own casenotes. In the course of their work, caseworkers build up a repository of information in the form of running casenotes and case summaries which can be used as evidence in the planned change effort. After all, it was this very casework experience which convinced the worker him- or herself of the need for reform. Casenotes are not often thought of by caseworkers, perhaps because the information seems too qualitative and disconnected to be useful. However, if casenotes are carefully probed for specific items of information, they can be used to make an emphatic case (see Barber, 1985). For example, the average length of time between occasions of service or the mean number of changes of address per year should be easy to extract from casenotes, yet both statistics could speak volumes about the clients' level of functioning in the community. As well as statistical data of this kind, casenotes provide an almost endless source of qualitative and anecdotal evidence; and carefully chosen anecdotes are among the most persuasive methods of convincing the public at large that a need exists. The mass media and the general public have no wish to wade through a morass of detail, no matter how convincing the figures. Unfortunately perhaps, they are more likely to respond to one or two emotive case examples than to complex and painstaking research. Without compromising client confidentiality, the worker should be prepared to exploit this public fascination with human interest stories.

*Survey approaches*

When social workers think of researching an issue, the survey is often the first strategy to spring to mind. There is no doubt that a carefully conducted survey can be another excellent method of establishing need but, as we shall see, surveys are often expensive and time-consuming, and the effort can be unjustifiable when the aim of the exercise is merely to establish that a need for change exists. Survey approaches to need assessment tend to fall into two categories. The first is the survey of existing community services and the second is the citizen survey. The first kind of survey provides information about help-seeking behaviour within a community, about gaps in services and about outreach and prevention efforts, while the second kind of survey is a valuable method of assessing community attitudes and opinions.

A survey of existing community services should begin by gathering information about the level of demand made on community agencies as well as the types of services that are demanded. Much of this information can be gleaned from agency reports or from the regular statistical returns that funding bodies usually require of welfare agencies. Where the information is not readily available, however, it may be necessary to resort to a brief, well-designed questionnaire. As well as the level and quality of demand, a community services survey describes the resources available to meet the demand. When combined with information about demand, a simple count of resources by type and capacity should enable the worker to identify gaps and make authoritative assertions about need. Naturally, the precise content of community services surveys will vary but Siegel, Attkison and Carson (1978) have identified the following general interest areas for inclusion in a survey of human service agencies within a geographical area:

1. Range of human services provided;

2. Client entry policies, conditions of eligibility for service, including age, sex, financial criteria, geographic restrictions, and particular focal or target population groups;

3. Personnel characteristics and personnel development efforts:
   a. Service providers by training and credentials,
   b. Provider training and continuing education opportunities,
   c. Treatment modalities provided,
   d. Number of individuals providing various services,
   e. Average client load per staff member;

4. Financial characteristics:
   a. Charge for services – fee schedule, eligibility for third party reimbursement, sliding scale provisions,
   b. Agency support – public or private, fees and other sources of funding categorized as percentage of total support budget;

5. Accessibility and availability of services, hours when services are provided, comfort and acceptability of the facility to the clients, and availability of child-care when necessary;

6. Referrals (demand):
   a. Number within a standardized time frame,
   b. Source categorized by service type or status of referring agent,
   c. Reasons (symptoms, problem areas),
   d. Other characteristics such as geographic locale or referring agents, geographic origin of clients who are referred, and temporal patterns of referrals;

7. Accepted for service:
   a. Number over a specified time period,
   b. Diagnosis or other nomenclature for designated problems,

    c. Sociodemographic characteristics of clients – age, race, sex, census tract, socioeconomic status,
    d. Those refused service and reasons for refusal;

8. Waiting list:
    a. Number of persons on waiting list,
    b. Reasons for waiting list,
    c. Symptoms or problem areas of individuals placed on waiting lists,
    d. Other characteristics, such as average time on waiting list and proportion of those placed on waiting list who do not eventually receive service;

9. Services provided:
    a. Human service problem areas thought to be of highest priority as well as services that are in increasing demand,
    b. Range of actual services provided categorized by units of service,
    c. List of referral resources that interface the agency,

10. Referrals initiated:
    a. Frequency of referrals made (listed across the range of agencies within the social area),
    b. Problems in making referrals – including such factors as transportation, financial, language, and cultural barriers. (pp. 235–6)

Where community surveys like this reveal that agencies are quite unable to meet the demands made on them, the worker clearly has valuable evidence of the need for additional resources. However, it must be borne in mind that a high level of demand for a service does not necessarily mean that the service itself is addressing an area of great importance within a community. It may be simply that the service is well known or one of the only services available. Indeed, information about the number of inappropriate cases referred to an agency can be used by the worker as an indicator of the inadequacy of services for a particular client group. Conversely, a service which is not well utilised may in fact be meeting a desperate need but factors such as strict admission criteria or poor publicity may prevent many clients from benefiting from the service. In other words, the same information can be used in different ways depending on the creativity of the worker who is interpreting it. As any politician knows, the real secret is not merely to have 'the facts' but to explore ways of interpreting them to your own advantage.

As well as community services surveys, citizen surveys of clients, professionals or the public at large can be another source of evidence. The basic methodological issues confronting anyone who embarks on a citizen survey are: (a) whom to ask, (b) what to ask, and (c) how to ask it. Let us briefly consider each issue in turn.

*Whom to ask.* The issue of whom to ask raises the potentially complex considerations involved in sampling. There are a number of ways of drawing samples and although a detailed discussion of sampling strategies is clearly beyond the scope of this book, it is useful at least to identify some of the sampling options open to workers engaged in transition work (as more comprehensive discussion of sampling is to be found in Kish, 1965). The basic distinction in sampling is between probability and non-probability samples, with probability samples being much more likely to result in a representative cross-section of community opinion. Probability sampling plans have the characteristic that every member of the population has a known probability of being chosen into the sample. This does not mean that every member of the population has the *same* probability of being chosen; rather, the chance that a group or individual will be selected is identical to its level of representation in the population as a whole. The basic probability sample is the 'simple random sample', in which all possible cases are assembled and selected entirely at random. For example, a simple random sample of a municipality would involve something akin to placing the names of every person in that municipality into a hat and drawing out names entirely at random; and it can be shown mathematically that this procedure enables the researcher to identify the opinions of the community as a whole. Another kind of probability sample is the stratified random sample, which involves dividing the population into two or more strata (such as males and females) and drawing a simple random sample from each stratum. A stratified random sample might be drawn when the researcher is interested in the views of certain minority groups of the population which would not be well represented if a simple random sample were drawn. A third probability sampling technique is known as multistage, or cluster, sampling. In cluster sampling, the researcher arrives at the ultimate set of respondents to be included in the sample by first sampling in terms of larger groupings or clusters. The clusters are selected by simple or stratified means. For example, a survey of urban households may take a sample of cities; and within each city, a sample of districts is selected; then within each district the final sample of households is drawn. At each stage, the samples are randomly selected. Thus the procedure moves from more inclusive to less inclusive sampling units until the final sample to be surveyed is attained.

Strictly speaking, only probability samples of the kind outlined above provide the basis for making statistical inferences to a population, but for the survey researcher without a great deal of time and effort to invest, probability sampling is often out of the question. Moreover, under our model, the social worker is unlikely to be interested in an unbiased assessment of overall community opinion. The worker will be more inclined to seek the opinions of the sub-group whose interests he or she represents and the opinions of people who are sympathetic to the sub-group. Under such circumstances a non-probability sampling strategy may suffice. As its name implies, a non-probability sample does not allow the researcher to determine the probability each respondent has of being selected and there can be no assurance that every respondent has some chance of selection. Since it is impossible to calculate the probability that one's sample differs from the population by more than a certain amount, one can not make unqualified statements about the community's views. Nevertheless, for reasons of convenience, non-probability sampling is the most frequently used strategy in the social sciences. Indeed, it is so common that most researchers ignore the need to qualify their conclusions and act as if they had drawn a truly representative sample anyway.

A common form of non-probability sampling is the 'accidental sample', in which the researcher simply reaches out and selects whoever comes to hand until the sample reaches a designated size. For example, the individual who stands on a street corner and interrogates passers-by in an effort to gauge public opinion is drawing an accidental sample and this kind of strategy clearly cannot guarantee representativeness. Nevertheless, it is often used by lobby groups more concerned about the absolute size of the sample than its representativeness, so if the sheer number of responses is all that counts (as in the number of people supporting a petition) a strategically chosen accidental sample can be sufficient.

Quota sampling is a second form of non-probability sampling but, unlike accidental sampling, it contains provisions to ensure that diverse elements of a population are included in the sample in the proportions in which they occur in the population. For example, if it is known that the population has equal numbers of males and females, the researcher surveys equal numbers of males and females. If it is known that 75 per cent of the population are blue-collar workers, the researcher ensures that 75 per cent of his or her sample are of this kind. Unlike stratified random sampling, in which all possible respondents within a certain stratum are identified before being selected randomly, the quota sampling strategy simply approaches individuals with the required characteristic until the predetermined quota is reached. For this reason, a quota sample is still basically an accidental sample conducted within each stratum. The researcher selects whoever comes to hand provided that the respondent satisfies the criterion (or criteria) for selection.

A third kind of non-probability sample is the purposive sample. The basic assumption of this strategy is that with good judgement and an appropriate strategy, the researcher can hand pick the cases to be sampled. Normally, this strategy involves identifying cases that the researcher judges to be typical of the population of interest. From a scientific point of view, it is clear that without an objective basis for making judgements, this strategy is not a dependable way of obtaining community opinion. However, more politically motivated researchers can exploit the imprecision of purposive sampling by selecting the worst cases they know of and acting as if they were typical. While it is impossible to prove that a purposive sample is typical of the population of interest, it can be just as hard to show that it is not. As with the anecdotal evidence gleaned from casenotes, information obtained from a mere handful of such carefully chosen 'typical' cases can be enough to convince the general public of the need for change. Resorting to anecdote in this way is a favourite tactic of politicians who use it to support claims that are difficult to disprove without effort and expense.

In summary, the worker's choice of sampling strategy must be determined by the resources that are available to conduct the survey as well as by the worker's purpose in conducting the survey in the first place. Where the worker has a genuine need to know something about a group of interest, he or she must define the population carefully and employ one of the more exacting probability sampling strategies. On the other hand, where workers are merely trying to gather evidence with which to influence popular opinion, less rigorous procedures will not only be easier, they may also be more politically astute.

*What to ask*. The field of survey research extends from totally unstandardised informal conversations at one extreme to highly structured questionnaires at the other. However, no matter how structured or unstructured they are, all surveys must satisfy three major prerequisites: accessibility, comprehensibility and motivation (cf. Lindzey and Aronson, 1968).

The accessibility requirement refers to the obvious point that a potential respondent has to possess the information wanted by the researcher: for example, there is clearly no point asking a respondent what his or her opinion of a local agency is if that respondent has never heard of the agency. Where researchers wish to ask questions of opinion or evaluation such as this, they should precede the question with an item that checks whether the respondent actually has the information needed to form an opinion. In some circumstances it can be appropriate to provide the information first and then ask for the respondent's opinion. Indeed, this tactic of supplying information before asking for an opinion is used by politically motivated researchers to make the desired result more likely. For example, the Australian federal government recently mounted a massive publicity campaign highlighting the enormous social cost of drug abuse and in this context it announced some aggressive and expensive drug prevention policies. The government then commissioned market researchers to survey public opinion about its anti-drug policies. Little wonder the vast majority of those surveyed applauded the government for its work! But what if the government had preceded its public opinion survey with information about the implications for other government programmes of pouring millions of dollars into drug prevention? By providing selective and leading information prior to asking opinion questions, the government was able to quote impressive statistics in support of itself.

The second prerequisite of survey research, comprehensibility, relates to the respondent's understanding of what constitutes an answer. The respondent must decide what is relevant information to give, how completely to answer, and in what terms to express the answer. Thus, it is part of the researcher's job to teach the respondent his or her role both in the initial explanation of the survey and in the way questions are asked and answers are treated. Questions should be phrased in simple, unambiguous language and, where any possible misunderstanding remains, an example can be given or the question asked in more than one way.

The third requirement for a successful interview is motivation on the part of the respondent to answer the questions accurately. This refers not only the respondent's decision to cooperate, but also to his or her motivation to give accurate answers. A recent survey conducted in North Queensland asked elderly people how much longer they expected to live! This is a rather gross example of the failure to take account of motivational issues when designing survey questions, and it is hardly surprising that when the necessary arithmetic was performed, it worked out that the projected average age at death was around 100 years! It is part of the researcher's job to reduce the effect of factors tending to decrease the level of motivation and build up the effect of those tending to increase it. Among the former are the desire to do other things, embarrassment at ignorance and dislike of the interview content, while the latter may include curiosity, politeness, a feeling of social responsibility, and so on.

Whether the question is one of opinion or 'fact', the researcher has a choice between open and pre-coded questions. In an open question the respondent is given freedom to decide the form and detail of his or her answer. In the case of pre-coded questions, either the respondent is given a limited number of answers from which to choose or the question is asked as an open question and the interviewer allocates the answer to the appropriate code category. The essential difference lies in the stage at which the information is coded, whether by the respondent or by the researcher. If the researcher prefers a detailed answer or wishes to find out what aspects of an issue are uppermost in the respondent's mind, it is preferable to leave the question open and allocate answers to categories later. This approach can be particularly appropriate for questions of opinion.

The advantages of pre-coded questions are evident. To combine the recording and coding of answers in one operation simplifies the whole procedure. If the range of answers to a question is obviously limited, pre-coding is preferable and most factual questions fall into this category. If however, one cannot reasonably determine in advance what the main categories will be, it is best to begin with open questions, progressing to pre-coded questions as the range and distribution of answers become clear. Inexperienced survey researchers sometimes make the mistake of pre-coding answers before they are certain of the full range of options. The answer to this pitfall – and it is a cardinal rule of survey design – is always to begin by conducting a pilot survey making liberal use of open-ended questions from which categories can be constructed later.

In addition to these general issues involved in questionnaire design, the following more specific tips are worth bearing in mind.

1. Be clear about precisely what information is needed and *keep the number of questions to a minimum*. The temptation is always to add more questions to the list. Long surveys detract from the motivational prerequisite outlined above and introduce an element of respondent fatigue that detracts from the quality of the information obtained.
2. Start with easy, non-threatening questions that build rapport. Keep more personal and potentially embarrassing matters until the survey is well under way.
3. Where the survey is long and tiring, keep easy questions (such as demographic details) until the end.
4. Always use simple, unambiguous language and avoid leading questions unless you fully intend to produce a certain result, as previously discussed.
5. Avoid pre-coding responses unless the question relates to straightforward factual matters or until pilot testing has established that the list of codes exhausts all possibilities. Even then, it can be useful to include an 'other' category for recording responses that do not quite fit into one of the pre-codes.
6. Where the question is complex or difficult to understand, ask it in more than one way or give an example.

In the end, however, designing survey questions remains a matter of common sense and experience; there are no theoretical rules which can be applied in a straightforward mechanical fashion (see Moser and Kalton, 1981, for a more thorough explanation of questionnaire construction).

*How to ask.* The final methodological issue confronting the survey researcher is how to go about obtaining information from respondents. Often the most satisfactory option is a face-to-face interview of all respondents selected into the sample. This method is likely to yield the highest response rate and ensures that the researcher remains in constant control of the sampling strategy. As one potential respondent drops out of the study for one reason or another, the researcher has the option of selecting another similar respondent to replace him or her. Another benefit of the

face-to-face interview is that the worker is able to monitor
the quality of the information supplied by the respondent
and clear up any misunderstandings on the spot. For
caseworkers who take on survey work in the course of all
their other duties, however, face-to-face interviews are
frequently impractical. They are expensive and time-consuming to conduct and they should only be contemplated when
the number of respondents is small or when additional
resources and personnel are available to support the exercise.

Another option is the postal survey, in which respondents
are selected according to a sampling strategy and dispatched
survey forms through the mail. This approach has a notoriously poor response rate, and postal surveyors can be
certain that only a minority will return completed questionnaires. Whether the worker is prepared to accept a poor
response rate largely depends on how important it is to have
a genuinely representative sample of community opinion and
this issue has already been discussed. If representativeness is
important, it can be useful to substitute a telephone survey or
to follow a postal survey with a follow-up telephone call.
However, telephone surveys tend to under-represent low
income earners (who are less likely to possess a telephone)
as well as the increasing number of individuals with unlisted
telephone numbers.

This brief overview of the survey approach to collecting
campaign evidence was undertaken primarily to alert caseworkers to the many issues involved in designing and
administering surveys. Once the survey has been completed,
the worker is then confronted with the task of analysing the
data; and it is here that survey research often founders
altogether. Unless the worker is clear from the outset about
how the information will be collated and analysed, it is better
not to embark on a survey at all.

*Community group approaches*

In addition to social indicators and surveys, there are various
community group approaches that can be employed by the
worker. Community group approaches have the advantage
of being relatively quick and inexpensive to undertake, and

their informality makes it more likely that unexpected options and information will be unearthed when compared with a survey. More than this, community group approaches can be used for the purpose of action research (that is, the use of the research process itself as part of the campaign for change).

In opting for a community group approach to need assessment, the researcher must choose between an open community forum or a more restrictive key-informant group. The choice is normally a tactical one which is related to the stage that has been reached in the campaign. Key-informant groups can be a most effective means of bringing people together into a core group, and this group would then call a public meeting to gather more information and increase support for the campaign.

*Community forums.* A community forum is an open meeting for all members of a designated group, be it a neighbourhood or a group of clients. Thus any person meeting basic membership requirements is potentially a source of information. Forums may include a wide range of activities including information exchange, discussion of some mutual problem, communication about government policy change, and so on. Clearly, the better the representation of all the elements within the community, the more satisfactory the end result. Community forums should therefore be undertaken only after extensive publicity and when it is likely that a large number of community members will actually be present.

Without question, the community forum is an economical means of gathering information. A large number of views and individual testimonials on an issue can be elicited without the labour-intensiveness of individual interviews. Related to this is the potential of the community forum to focus sharply the different views that may exist within the community. However, the community forum clearly cannot guarantee that all opinions will be heard. For this reason, they are inappropriate when the worker needs a representative summary of community opinion. Probably the most attractive feature of the community forum is that it can provide a catalyst for a campaign of social action. Public meetings of this kind are key instruments in the Alinskyist tactic of fanning any hostility that exists within the community in order to motivate political activity. Moreover, leaders are likely to emerge who can be conscripted into the campaign.

*Key-informant groups.* The establishment of a key-informant group to provide information around a circumscribed issue (for example, lack of child care, inadequate aftercare for psychiatric patients or lengthy public housing waiting lists) is another useful way of launching a campaign and collecting evidence at the same time. In this approach certain key individuals are approached and asked to participate in a small group forum to help the worker gather information and opinions about some problem or issue. At the earliest group meetings it is sensible to have a structured and non-threatening procedure for eliciting information and promoting group discussion. One such procedure is Delbecq and Van de Ven's (1977) nominal group technique. This model was developed primarily to help planning groups define problems clearly and develop programmes to solve those problems. In its original form the model contains five basic phases: problem exploration, knowledge exploration, priority development, programme development and programme evaluation. The term *nominal* group comes from the fact that, although individuals are divided into small groups of six to nine people, much of the work is done alone.

For our present purposes (where the group is not a policy-making body), the nominal group technique could be modified to include three basic steps: problem exploration, priority development and brainstorming solutions. After introducing participants and the group itself, the worker would ask everyone to spend some time listing aspects of the problem as they experience it. Either the worker or a volunteer from the group then collates these lists and some time is spent clarifying, elaborating and adding items. Next, each member is asked to work alone to rank items in order of their importance to him or her. It is not always necessary to develop a group priority list but time should be spent discussing individual rankings. Finally, the brainstorming technique described in Chapter 4 would be used to identify potential solutions to the group's plight. As well as raising the prospect of collective action, this procedure will obviously generate qualitative evidence that can be used later in the planned change effort.

In summary, the transition to the community organisation phase of our model involves the worker in: (a) bringing individual clients together into an informal support and discussion group, and (b) gathering evidence in support of the need for policy change. Higher system level activity of the kind described in Chapter 1 begins in earnest when the informal group is transformed into a people's organisation committed to a campaign of social action. In the next chapter we will consider some of the more important steps involved in launching a successful campaign.

# 7

# Practical Issues in Forming an Organisation and Mounting a Campaign

In the previous chapter we looked at the formation of client support groups as a precursor to formal organisations dedicated to a programme of social action. In this chapter we turn our attention to the practicalities involved in building the organisation and mounting the campaign. In moving from support group to lobby group, a client group will need to take account of at least four basic considerations: (a) how to plan and market its ideas; (b) how to formalise the organisation; (c) how to obtain resources; and (d) how to lobby decision-makers. Although we will discuss each of these issues in turn, it is worth stating at the outset that community organisation of this kind does not progress neatly from one step to the next, and activity often proceeds on all four fronts at once.

## Planning and marketing a campaign

Community organisers may feel uncomfortable with the suggestion, but the fact is that a client group which decides to embark on a campaign is immediately faced with what is essentially a marketing problem: how can we get certain key people to do what we want? In this sense a client group is not fundamentally different from any other sectional interest (including business interest) in the marketplace; like them it competes for hearts and minds. For this reason, some of the basic principles of market research can be very helpful to client groups in the early stages of planning a campaign. The first principle of successful marketing is to be clear about precisely what it is that the group wants to achieve and how it intends to go about it. Hunter (1984) has proposed the following checklist for community groups to help them achieve clarity on these fundamental issues.

1. Who are we, what do we do, and why do we do it?
2. Who is affected by what we want to do?
3. What target group are we trying to reach?
4. What do we want the target group to do? What is in it for them?
5. How do we reach them? Where are they? How can we contact them? What do we say?
6. How do we follow through? What happens when people do what we want? What stops people doing what we ask? How do we check that we delivered what we promised? (p. 2)

According to Hunter (1984), a group is only ready to launch a campaign when it is capable of answering all these questions clearly and succinctly. It can be useful to employ a structured procedure such as the nominal group technique discussed in Chapter 6 or the problem-solving procedure outlined in Chapter 4 to help members resolve these issues. Because there are usually many ways of achieving aims, whatever procedure is used the group must take care to canvass all programme options before selecting the one which seems best for it. Having identified all the options, each programme can be plotted on a simple matrix such as the one shown in Figure 7.1.

Clearly, the ideal programme will be one which combines a high level of importance with a low degree of difficulty but, consistent with the principles outlined in Chapter 3, fledgeling client groups comprised of marginalised individuals would be better advised to embark on easier options first and plan to confront more difficult challenges after experiencing one or two successes.

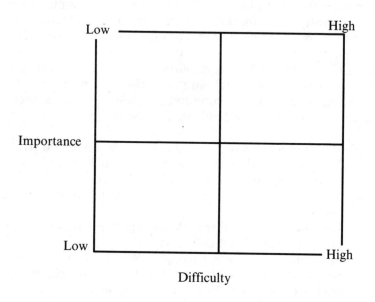

**Figure 7.1**    *An example of a simple programme planning matrix*

A related marketing technique that can be applied in the early stages of organisation development is so-called SWOT analysis (Kotler, 1975). SWOT is an acronym that stands for strengths, weaknesses, opportunitiestes and threats. Together these terms direct the group to look for programs which build on the group's strengths, compensate for its weaknesses, make the most of its opportunities, and guard against threats to group objectives. Thus, group members begin the SWOT process by identifying all the strengths of the organisation: for example, the group may encompass certain skills or knowledge, or perhaps a considerable amount of free time. On the other hand, a new client group is certain to have weaknesses in relation to its objectives, such as a lack of resources or limited expertise in lobbying and community organising. These weaknesses should also be listed. Next, opportunities provided by the outside world in relation to achieving one or more of the programmes are considered: for example, a special connection with a journalist, community leader or someone else who can help. Finally, the group tries to anticipate outside threats to the campaigns under consideration. When the group is clear about what it is doing and why, it is desirable to write it all down in a short, clear case statement. The case statement projects the kind of image the group wants and can be used to publicise the group's objectives.

Having clarified its programmes, the group should proceed to identify its target group(s). Marketers have proved repeatedly that campaigns are more likely to succeed when a target person or group is selected and the campaign is directed primarily at that person or group. By selecting a specific target, the group can tailor its campaign to achieve maximum effect on the individuals identified. In the slick jargon of commercial marketers, target groups can be identified by a process of 'market segmentation by demographics, geographics and psychographics' (Hunter, 1984). This simply means defining target groups according to *who* they are (perhaps politicians or civil servants), *where* they are (such as constituency, organisation or neighbourhood) and *what* interests them. Even if the community group wants to reach as broad a range of people as possible, its campaign is still more likely to be effective if the group can pick two or three different target groups within the range and direct its message to these sub-groups.

Having clarified its objectives, canvassed the various campaign options and identified the targets necessary to ensure success, the group now must consider what the various target groups have to gain *and lose* by doing what it wants them to do. The group stands a much better chance of success if it understands the target group's point of view. Because of their commitment to the cause community groups often make the mistake of feeling that everyone else ought to feel the same way they do. But people make choices based on what is important to them, so the group needs to consider what is likely to be important about the issue from the target group's point of view. For example, politicians have a responsibility to their parties to win votes, newspaper editors must print stories that people will actually read, and unemployed volunteers are likely to want good work experience, not just the chance to become involved in a good cause.

For a client group embarked on a campaign of social reform, it is almost inevitable that market research will reveal one or more of its targets to be unsympathetic but it is sometimes possible to reframe the group's objectives to make them more consistent with the attitudes of the target group. For example, an Indo-Chinese refugee association in Australia was having no success in lobbying the federal government to accept greater numbers of refugees for resettlement in Australia during the 1970s because politicians were fearful of a backlash from Australia's notoriously anti-Asian voting public. After reconsidering their marketing strategy, the association decided not to lobby directly for an increased refugee intake but to promote the Australian idea, 'give the underdog a fair go'. This new marketing strategy had the effect of increasing Australia's refugee intake almost immediately. However, where interests simply cannot be reconciled and conflict between the client group and one or more of its targets is inevitable, the most powerful tool for getting what the clients want will normally be media pressure and the issue of attracting media attention will be discussed later in the chapter.

### Formalising the group

Having done its market research and adopted a case statement which is descriptive of its aims and objectives, the group is in a position to draft a constitution. Not all community groups will require a constitution, of course. Groups which grow up around a single, short-lived issue or which have a small, informal membership which owns nothing in common and has no need of income are examples of groups which may not need a formal constitution. However, a constitution is necessary if the group is to become a legally incorporated body and this has a number of potential benefits for people's organisations. A legally incorporated association can own land and other assets in its own name instead of in the names of members or trustees. It can also make contracts and have them enforced legally, and it usually has limited liability if it runs into debt. Limited liability protects individual group members from being sued and is especially important if the group runs any risk of accidents which might result in a public liability claim. Because an unincorporated body has no separate legal existence apart from the individual members, a legal liability incurred by the group (such as rent on premises or an accident not covered by insurance) will probably result in group members being personally responsible for the debts. Another compelling reason for incorporating is that government funding bodies will not normally provide grants to unincorporated groups because of the uncertainty about how the money will be administered and accounted for. Constitutions specify procedures for financial accountability, auditing and the steps to be followed should the organisation wind up or become insolvent. A final reason for incorporating is because some groups may be eligible to register as a charity, making them exempt from various taxes themselves and enabling benefactors to deduct donations from their taxable income.

Although the precise details of constitutions vary according to the legislation governing associations and the sorts of management structure provided by the legislation, all constitutions need to cover similar topics (Halliday, 1980). Among the more important are the name and objectives of the organisation, its membership categories and qualifications, responsibilities of its office-bearers, its decision-making structure and voting procedures, and its financial management procedures. Although constitutions are technical documents which are difficult, if not impossible, for people without legal training to draw up, model constitutions are normally held by the government department responsible for registering associations and these models can be adapted to suit the needs of most client groups without having to engage a solicitor.

Soon after making the decision to mount a campaign a new client group will often want to expand its support base. The most common means of launching a group's campaign and of recruiting new members at the same time is to call a public meeting. It is not usually necessary to have a formal constitution before launching the organisation at a public meeting but, where this has already been done, the constitution should be circulated and ratified at the meeting. Careful planning of the group's first public meeting is vital (cf. Lathey, 1974; Community Action, 1975; H. M. Taylor and Mears, 1976; Norton, 1977; Community Liaison, 1978; Henderson and Thomas, 1980; Clancy, 1981). This is a particularly vulnerable stage in the group's life and a poorly attended or disorganised public meeting can result in group members becoming discouraged and giving up altogether.

Prior to the meeting the group must sort out who is going to do what, agree on what each person is going to say and on the role of the chairperson, order of speakers, and so on. If the group wants resolutions to be discussed and approved at the public meeting, the various options should be fully discussed by the group before the public meeting. However, it is also important to remember that while there will be people in the audience who will be relying on the organisers for guidance, whatever resolutions are formulated should reflect the wishes of the people present, and this may result in the organisers having to modify their thinking. The timing of the meeting can be vital. The group should ensure that the meeting does not conflict with popular television programmes or other events – such as late night shopping or sporting events – which could keep people from attending. The meeting place itself must be convenient for as many people as possible and, where applicable, held in the locality most affected by the issues under discussion. The hall should not be so large that the meeting could not possibly fill it as this can have an adverse effect on the morale of participants.

The date of the meeting must allow sufficient time for publicity, and leaflets and press releases should be prepared for distribution. The leaflets should not only give information about where and when the meeting is being held, they should also explain why the meeting is being held and why the issue is so important. It would be wise also to include a contact address and telephone number and distribute the leaflets no later than five to seven days before the meeting. Enough notice must be given for people to make arrangements, but not so much notice that people will forget. More advance notice can be given through local newspapers, posters left in public places and through radio and television press releases.

At the beginning of the meeting a chairperson needs to be elected and this is normally done by having a member of the organising committee nominate someone whom the committee has decided on in advance. If the group already has a president this step can be skipped but, if the group genuinely wishes to launch a new people's organisation at the meeting, it is preferable at least to get the meeting's endorsement of the core group's committee structure. The nomination for chairperson is seconded and any objections to the nominated person are called for. Obviously the chairperson needs to be someone who is capable of running a meeting, especially when the group is new. Once the chairperson has been chosen, he or she should quickly assume responsibility for getting the meeting under way. If an agenda has been prepared, copies should be distributed at this stage and suggestions taken by the chairperson for changes or additions to the items. A person should also be elected (or simply nominated) to take the minutes of the meeting.

Where a constitution is already in existence, the chairperson must be familiar with it and abide by the rules of the association as specified in the constitution. He or she then opens the meeting and explains what it is about before introducing each speaker in turn. The chairperson directs the meeting by controlling question time, steering questions to those people who can answer them and ensuring that everyone gets a chance to speak. He or she must also keep the meeting moving through its agenda, focus contributions on the point under discussion, summarise discussion on each agenda item as it is completed and summarise the whole meeting at the end. Most public meetings fall roughly into three phases:

1. *beginning*, including a welcoming statement, an explanation for calling the meeting, and statements by a member

of the core group on the present position and future
action hoped for;

2. *middle*, during which there are speeches by others
(especially people of some appeal or notoriety), and the
meeting is opened to the floor for comment or discussion;

3. *end*, during which suggestions and resolutions for action
are considered and voted on, appeals for support,
membership or money are made, and future meetings
are planned.

The meeting is not over when it closes. Someone from the
organising committee should have circulated a sheet for
those attending to record their names, addresses and
telephone numbers and a copy of the minutes should be
sent to all those who attended. These same people can also be
sent all relevant literature and requests for assistance
prepared by the organising committee from then on. If the
meeting was unsuccessful, the organisers should meet to
discuss why. There may have been a poor turnout or a
hostile or apathetic audience and these reactions may have
had something to do with the way the meeting was
conducted. Under these circumstances, the group may
decide to concentrate on some of the other means of
lobbying and attracting attention to their campaign that
will be discussed later in this chapter.

### Obtaining funds

It is never long before a new community group comes up
against the problem of money. If the group has not already
incurred expenses in staging its public meeting, it will soon
feel the need for salaries, accommodation, printing, station-
ery, postage and other resources to enable it to function. As
well as approaching philanthropic trusts and private companies willing to give a tax deductible donation (assuming the
group has succeeded in incorporating as a tax deductible
association), a fledgeling community group will often have to
turn to government to provide an operating grant. Governments hand out millions of dollars to community groups

every year and, from the government's perspective, there are several good reasons for doing so. Sometimes community groups can provide services more cheaply or efficiently than the government itself. Community groups can also try innovative ideas without committing the government to anything. Finally, governments usually have a philosophical commitment to encouraging community participation and self-help in the area of social services.

All government departments which dispense funds have developed guidelines about whom and what to fund. Thus the first step in applying for funding is to find out exactly what a government department is prepared to fund. The group should draw up a list of potential government grants and funding bodies and establish exactly what the purpose of each funding programme is. For example, is there a particular target group (such as women or migrants), function (for instance, information centres or respite care), or way of operating (such as self-help) which is favoured by the funding body? If so, the group should seek to satisfy some or all of these preferred characteristics, even if it means modifying its original ideas. In addition, it is important to know how the money is apportioned. There may be a maximum grant or strict guidelines about precisely what is funded: for example, some guidelines preclude expenditure on capital works, and others on salaries; still other grants require that the group itself raise a certain proportion of the funds. The timing of the grant is another important variable to clarify. Some funding programmes receive submissions all year round and pay out immediately, while others make allocations for a calendar or financial year with a deadline for applications several months in advance. Whatever documentation exists about funding guidelines should be obtained and the individuals responsible for administering the grant should be contacted and asked for their advice and assistance in preparing a submission.

Although there inevitably will be differences in the detail of various types of funding application, there are general guidelines that should be adhered to by every group preparing a submission. Most importantly, the group must cover the fundamental issues of *what* is wanted, *why* it is wanted, and *how much* it will cost (J. Taylor, 1984; Victorian Council of Social Service, 1985). Depending on what the grant is for, the group may also need to explain how the funded programme will be managed and evaluated. The presentation of these issues should display a logical and orderly arrangement of ideas. The application begins with a simple and unambiguous heading or title on the front page. The same page should carry information about whom the submission comes from, to whom it is directed, and under what funding programme. Where the submission is a large one, the next page should carry a table of contents. The body of the submission normally begins with a brief description of its purpose, including its operational objectives. In other words, the group must state what it hopes to achieve with the money and why, paying particular attention to the need to relate these objectives to the objectives of the funding programme. These objectives should be supported by a need assessment and the reader is referred back to Chapter 6 for a discussion of methods for establishing need. Where possible, the operations of the group should be related to gaps in existing facilities or services, and it is always impressive to refer to statistics that indicate the extent of the problem. It can be a good idea to obtain statements of support from representatives of local organisations and government departments. As well as the support of professionals in the field, evidence should be provided that the prospective target group represented by the applicants agrees with the objectives of the submission. In regard to this latter point, it can be useful to supply quotes from the public meeting or details of any questionnaires or discussion groups conducted during the transition phase discussed earlier.

After covering the issues of what is wanted and why, the group is ready for the most daunting section of the funding submission: the budget. The first step in preparing a budget is to identify all the group's activities that will cost money. It is useful to prepare a checklist, with each major activity across the top of the page and types of income and expenses down the side. Having established what items need to be covered, a financial worksheet can then be made up for each item. The aim of the worksheet is to produce a detailed estimate of the cost of each item. Where possible, the estimates for each item should be phased in according to the time of the year that it becomes payable. For example, in preparing an estimate of the cost of a telephone, the group would estimate the number of calls that would be expected in a given period and the cost of renting the telephone, in addition to the times of year that the telephone bill is payable. The reason for calculating phased costings is because funding bodies rarely provide the entire grant in a lump sum; instead, they provide the money in equal instalments or in response to an estimate for the forthcoming quarter. An example of a phased financial worksheet for telephone expenses is shown in Figure 7.2.

---

**Item**: Telephone expenses

**Notes**: Based on an estimate of 20 calls per week throughout the year, and rent of $65 payable quarterly.


$137                    $137                    $137                    $137

---

JAN. FEB. MAR. APR. MAY. JUN. JUL. AUG. SEP. OCT. NOV. DEC.

---

**Figure 7.2**  *Financial worksheet*


Having gone through the process of completing a worksheet for each item of expense and income, the information is summarised in a summary budget showing the totals for all activities. There are many ways of drawing up a summary budget (cf. Baird, 1985) and the precise format is pretty much a matter of personal taste. However, an example of a typical summary budget is shown in Figure 7.3.

| Item | Amount |
|------|-------:|
| *Expenses* | |
| Salary | 30 000 |
| 15% salary on-costs (i.e. superannuation, insurance, etc.) | 4 500 |
| Telephone | 900 |
| Postage and stationary | 350 |
| Transport for worker | 500 |
| Printing of brochures, etc. | 750 |
| Rent of office space | 7 000 |
| Office equipment | 10 000 |
| Audit | 350 |
| *Total expenses* | 54 350 |
| *Income* | |
| Membership fees | 1 000 |
| Donations | 3 000 |
| Grant required | 50 350 |
| *Total income* | 54 350 |
| *Balance at end of year* | *NIL* |

**Figure 7.3**   *Summary budget*

After costing the project, the funding submission should explain how the project will be managed. At this point, reference can be made to the management structure enshrined in the constitution. Lines of responsibility should be designated along with a description of management practices, such as membership and scheduling of project review meetings, and the mechanics of financial management and accountability. As part of the management process, the group should also describe how it intends to evaluate progress.

Throughout the process of completing a submission, the group must be aware of the need to gain support for its application. The best way to persuade the funding body to accept a submission is not normally by direct lobbying but by pre-selling the group's ideas to the administrators who make recommendations on which submissions should be successful. If the group starts as recommended earlier by contacting administrators at least once to ask their advice and discuss the group's ideas, the process of persuading decision-makers will have begun already. Getting evidence of support for the group's proposal from a range of users and local organisations will also help to sell the project. As well as establishing the need for a programme and improving the group's credibility, the support of others will show that voters care about the proposal going ahead. A final thing to try can be a press release (see below) about the group's activities in which the fact is mentioned that a funding submission has been made to support the group's objectives. Direct lobbying for the submission by contacting politicians, departmental managers or the people who sit on the committee that makes the funding decisions must be handled tactfully (Victorian Council of Social Service, 1981). While such a strategy can be influential, some decision-makers resent direct approaches from applicants and the civil servants who make the recommendations may be annoyed to find that a group has gone over their heads in an effort to influence the decision. Rather than asking for a decision in its favour it is often safer for the group to ask decision-makers for help or advice on an aspect of its submission.

Although the vast majority of grants are made under an established funding programme to submissions which comply with funding guidelines, there are some occasions when a community group can go outside established funds. When the request is very modest or very innovative, for example, ministers will sometimes direct civil servants to make an *ex gratia* payment. In addition, some funding programmes are left with money unexpectedly at the end of their financial year, perhaps because a programme has been cancelled. At such times, an interesting proposal for just the right sum may be funded informally to avert the danger of the funding body having its own allocation reduced in the next financial year.

In addition to funding its various activities, a newly-established community group seeking to change social policy in some way must be prepared to draw public attention to its cause. However, as this process of attracting media attention and lobbying is often intended to embarrass or confront policy-makers it is sensible to secure funding before mounting a concerted publicity campaign. Indeed, one of the ways that governments control criticism of themselves is through the regulation of grants to community groups, so it is essential that a new community group give consideration to its financial needs before embarking on the next stage: mounting a publicity campaign.

## Lobbying decision-makers

Probably the most effective way of putting pressure on politicians and decision-makers is to publicise the group's campaign through the media, but it is important for the group to realise that news coverage does not just happen. The vast majority of stories and news items are covered only because someone has taken the trouble to notify the media and *make* the story happen. Moreover, client groups must compete with hundreds of other sectional interests which contact the media every day in an effort to get their messages across. Thus, a newly-formed people's organisation needs to plan its strategy carefully if it is to succeed in having its issue covered.

The first and most important step in the process is for the group to clarify (and often simplify) what it wants to appear in the media. Too many community groups make the mistake of contacting the media before thinking their message through. This is almost certain to result in misunderstanding and misrepresentation of the group's cause. It can be easy enough to attract media publicity if the group is prepared to do something dramatic, such as occupying the local offices of the public housing authority, but such a gesture will be to no avail if the group is unable to state within a very brief period of time what it wants and why. A standard television news interview runs for approximately 30 seconds, so a good test of the group's readiness for media attention is whether or not its spokesperson is able to state the case within that period of time. Of course, decisions about what to say and how to say it will depend on which section of the media the group is targeting. Where possible group members should spend a month or so simply monitoring newspapers, magazines, and radio and television programmes for items or causes which are similar to its own. This will enable the group to identify relevant journalists and become acquainted with the kinds of stories that are likely to get coverage in which sections of the media.

Having decided on its basic strategy, the client group has a number of options for contacting the media. Brief messages, such as a news tip, request for an interview or invitation to an event can be given by telephone to the chief of staff or relevant journalist of a large newspaper, to the editor of a small newspaper, the news editor of a radio or television newsroom, or the producer of a current affairs or human interest show. Where a client group is interested in television coverage, it is imperative that consideration be given to the visual possibilities of the story. Television has an insatiable appetite for action, yet groups seeking publicity often contact television reporters merely requesting an interview. Television reporters prefer to restrict interviews to important or public figures, so it is better for the group to think of a story angle that ensures action scenes if it wants a television crew to cover it.

Needless to say, the telephone is not an appropriate vehicle for transmitting more complex messages. Under these circumstances it is advisable either to invite a reporter to meet with the group or, preferably, for the group to write a media release. A media release is a news item or story which is written as closely as possible to the style in which it would be reported in a newspaper or read on radio or television news. It can be used by a newly-formed community group either to make an announcement (such as announcing a public meeting or protest march) or to launch a campaign (perhaps calling on the government to create more child care places in the area). Because a media release can be wholly or partially inserted into a newspaper or news broadcast, it requires little effort on the part of journalists to make it into a newsworthy item. Indeed, it is a matter of conventional wisdom within newspaper circles that the best way to get a journalist to write a story about you is to write it yourself. But whatever may be the benefits to the journalist, a well written media release ensures that the group's cause is reported accurately because the issues are presented in the group's own words.

Media releases should be typed, double-spaced and limited to a single page with the names and telephone numbers of at least two contact people on the bottom of the sheet. If possible, the page should contain a recognisable letterhead so that the reader can tell at a glance what the writer's affiliation is. The report should also begin with the kind of headline that the group would like to see used in a newspaper article on the subject. Newspaper articles are sometimes shortened literally by chopping off the last few sentences so it is vital that the most important points be placed in the opening few sentences. But even where a media release escapes the sub-editor's scissors, many readers will not listen or read past the first few lines anyway. Thus, a media release needs to be capable of being read and understood quickly, with each sentence able to stand on its own. Colourful quotes make the material more interesting to reporters. It does not much matter who is quoted (the writer him- or herself will do), as long as the quote is attributed to a particular person, giving full name, title and position in the organisation. For example, a quote such as: 'A spokesperson for the group, Ms. Jenny Owen, said "No-one in the government cares what happens to us. We're just numbers on a list to them" ', could liven up a media release dealing with a client group's campaign for a new service in its neighbourhood. The media are always on the lookout for human interest stories as well as items that are colourful or sensational, so the group must learn to play up these angles rather than rely on dry discourse, no matter how valid the case may be. It is also worth remembering that a story of marginal interest to news executives will have more chance of getting a run in a newspaper if it is accompanied by a picture. It is advisable, therefore, to include a black and white photograph with a media release and on the back of the photograph there should be a caption naming the people and saying what they are doing, where and when. Finally, if the timing of the statement is important, this should appear at the top of the page: for example, 'For immediate release', or 'Embargoed until Friday, 4 April'.

On the issue of timing a media release, it is important to realise that *when* a news item is released can be vital to its chances of being accepted: the time of year, day of the week, and even time of day can all play a role. For instance, it is easier to have a story covered on public holidays or during the Christmas–New Year period because more people on holidays means less competition for space. Radio and television will also run 'light' stories on Saturdays and Sundays because there is less 'hard' news to report. It can thus be a good tactic to embargo a media release until a quiet day so that the story is given its best chance of getting a run. If all else fails it is perfectly acceptable to call on newspapers and radio and television stations in person. It is harder for reporters to ignore someone who is sitting in front of them than it is to file a media release in the waste paper basket.

As well as telephone calls, media releases and personal visits, calling a press conference is another way of attracting media attention. The press conference simply involves calling media people together to meet someone who has something to tell them. This approach will only be successful if (a) the issue is big news, or (b) the person is big news, so if at least one of these conditions is not satisfied it is pointless calling a press conference because the media representatives will not arrive. If the group's cause is not interesting to the general public, the group needs to seek out a sponsor who is capable of attracting publicity. A sympathetic sports star, musician or media personality would do nicely. The press conference can then be called by sending invitations to the media executives nominated earlier, asking them to send a representative. Supplementary invitations can be sent to any reporters who might be interested. The meeting should be at a time and place which suits as many media people as possible; it can help to check in advance with a reporter to ensure that the conference does not clash with a big event. The invitation should contain brief information on the person who is to be interviewed and if possible some indication of news interest, pointing up the angle the group wants the media to explore. The invitations need to arrive one or two days before the conference and should be followed up by a telephone call. A press conference is normally started with a brief statement from the group's spokesperson before throwing the forum open to questions. Once again, it is imperative that the spokesperson has worked out what to say in advance and is able to say it succinctly. Handing out a one-page background or information sheet can be useful.

If the group succeeds in getting an article in the newspaper, the story should be followed up with several letters to the editor written by group members without disclosing their association with the group. Newspapers like to think they are stirring up interest in an issue and letters to the editor are taken to be a reliable indicator of the interest level. The group should also look for another angle for a follow-up article and telephone talk-back radio to discuss the issue because communication is most effective when the message is directed at the target group several times in several different ways.

If, despite the group's best efforts, its overtures to the media are not taken up, it is worth persisting. Media releases can be re-written slightly and submitted at another time, or they can be put in the form of a letter to the editor. It is not always necessary to seek coverage in the mass media, however. Particularly when the issue is a local one, it can be more fruitful for the group to launch the campaign at the local level and develop a groundswell of support before seeking to broaden the issue any further.

It is also worth remembering that a media campaign is not the group's only option for bringing pressure to bear on decision-makers. For example, lobbyists estimate that somewhere between ten and thirty letters on a topic to one politician represent a groundswell of opinion to the receiver (Hunter, 1984). The best letters are personal and direct; form letters are much less persuasive. Needless to say, letter campaigns work best on marginal seat holders so, where possible, it is desirable for letters to emanate from marginal electorates. The most direct approach to a decision-maker is to write a brief letter giving background information about the issue and the group, and then to telephone to arrange a meeting. The meeting should be carefully planned: a leader should be selected to give the introduction and summary, and other members should each have one point to make. The group must be specific about facts and what it is asking the decision-maker to do. Requests must be practical and this will depend on factors such as whether the request will lose votes, cost too much, require legislative change, and so on. The group therefore needs to think about the likely reactions of the decision-maker and be prepared for all possible objections. After the delegation, a follow-up letter should be sent summarising the points made and what the group wants done.

A newly-formed client group may also consider direct confrontation as a way of publicising its cause and pressuring decision-makers, but such tactics can only ever be part of a larger programme aimed at achieving the group's goals. Plans for direct action must therefore consider not only the immediate impact of a particular activity but its likely effect on other parts of the campaign as well. Before involving itself in direct action, the group should familiarise itself with its legal rights. Some of the tactics to be covered are likely to be illegal and group members should know what they are getting into and move to protect themselves from legal retribution as far as possible. Civil liberties groups will provide the necessary advice.

One of the most common direct action tactics is a march or procession aimed at calling attention to the group and its cause. In most places in the Western world marches are legal as they consist mainly of people using their legal right to move along a roadway. Nevertheless, the local council and police should be notified in writing of the march, stating time, date and route. The march may be considered likely to obstruct the traffic, and the police can order dispersion. Normally for an obstruction to be an offence, however, there must be an unreasonable use of the roadway, taking into account the time of day, amount of traffic, width of road and number of people present. Of course, the group may also decide that it wants to jam or block access to certain places: for example, forming large queues of pseudo-purchasers at a department store or parking cars so that a street has to be closed can be a highly successful way of attracting attention. Technically, blocking a street or interfering with normal trade is an offence but this need not result in prosecution; much will depend on factors such as the number of protesters involved, the amount of media coverage achieved, and how well organised the demonstration is. When planning the route for a march it is also important to give consideration to how and where it will end. Rather than fizzle out, a march should proceed to a public place of sufficient space to allow a public meeting or demonstration to occur.

As well as marches and demonstrations, the group might also consider disruption or sabotage tactics (cf. Alinsky, 1969, 1971; Piven and Cloward, 1977). Examples of these strategies include disrupting a local government meeting at which a contentious matter is being discussed, acquiring a single share in a public company in order to attend and disrupt an annual shareholders' meeting, or protesting inside a large shopping centre against certain products or forms of advertising. The use of such tactics should obviously be limited and focused on a particular organisation; repeated or indiscriminate use of these tactics may become counter-productive.

Particularly in situations where the group is pressing for the provision of a new service or increased spending on some public utility, it can be a powerful gesture to take over an area of public land or occupy an empty office or house. Once the land or dwelling is occupied and a just case is established for its use, it can even be difficult for a public authority to evict the group. Sit-ins in government offices, local councils and company offices can also be a powerful symbolic gesture, but such action is invariably illegal and can bring swift police retaliation. For this reason, surprise is a necessary part of the strategy and the group should be able to make its point quickly. Because direct action tactics like these are intended to draw attention to the group's cause, it is obviously imperative that the group notify the media of such events by way of a media release.

In summary, client groups that decide to embark on a political campaign, no matter how limited in scope, need to give consideration to the practical issues involved in planning and marketing, legal incorporation, obtaining funding and lobbying. There is no sure recipe for success, but the group will maximise its chances through careful planning and painstaking attention to detail. Even the most spontaneous-looking demonstrations require careful organisation and timing if they are to be successful. Through all this planning the worker should be on hand to provide advice and encouragement but, as the work proceeds, he or she must become less of a leader and more of a resource person.

# 8

# Putting It Together

## Review

The approach to practice developed in these pages conceives of casework as a stage in a more comprehensive social work intervention. It is a process model of practice in which the practitioner's casework experience eventually drives the intervention beyond the level of individual 'cases' to organised client groups engaged in social action on their own behalf. This movement from casework to community organisation is unlikely to occur in the course of a single case because it relies on an understanding of the immediate socio-political problems uniting a population of clients. Indeed, the community organising activities described in the latter part of the book may take many 'cases', spread over months or years, to emerge fully.

The point of entry into our model, the social assessment, is vital if our approach is to be operationalised properly. As we saw in Chapter 1, precisely how the assessment is conducted will determine whether or not the practitioner ever moves beyond Phase I of our model. Caseworkers who adopt not merely the jargon but also the reality of social work's holistic view of human problems cannot help but be impressed sooner or later by the broader social forces implicated in their casework practice. While engaged in Phase I (individual–mesosystem) activity, the holistic caseworker comes to understand that broader social change is desirable, even essential, if the client's problem is to be addressed satisfactorily. This realisation normally follows the repeated and

122

frustrating experience of being able to provide only partial solutions through casework alone.

Traditional casework proclaims the primacy of the individual and asserts the importance of striving for solutions that take account of every client's idiosyncratic predicament (Meyer, 1987). By contrast, our approach encourages practitioners to look for commonalities in clients' circumstances, for it is the existence of common problems that alerts both worker and client to the broader systemic forces which underlie and sustain individual problems. When these common themes are understood, social work begins to move beyond Phase I and into what we have referred to as the transition phase. During this phase, the worker (if not yet the client) has some understanding of what changes are needed at the exosystem level, and he or she begins the process of social action. The caseworker has two vital assets with which to conduct the campaign. First, the worker has contacts with clients and their 'significant others'. These individuals not only legitimise the campaign, they drive it. When clients are brought together and their individual concerns collectivised, their demands are given force and urgency. The voice of a well organised client group can be very difficult for policy-makers to ignore, especially when the group is able to attract sympathetic media attention. Second, the caseworker has tangible evidence of the need for change. As discussed in Chapter 6, when this evidence is collated and systematised, the organisation is ready to launch its campaign publicly.

The movement from client support group to People's Organisation is the focus of activity in the third, or community organisation, phase of our model. By this time, the worker will have moved from the level of casework through group work to community organisation. This movement of clients from isolated and marginalised individuals to members of an assertive client organisation is arguably the most difficult task of all to achieve under our model. The process is one of empowerment and, although there is no magic formula for achieving it, we have looked at the psychological principles which inform practice in this regard.

It must be re-emphasised that although ours is a process model of practice, it is not a rigidly linear one. The social work perspective on human problems is necessarily complex and the practitioner's understanding of all the factors involved is likely to undergo modification as more cases are encountered and more is learned about social policy through involvement in social action. Indeed, most case-workers will be required to continue receiving cases while transition and community organisation work is in progress. This point brings us to an oft-heard objection to caseworkers becoming involved in social action: the sheer weight of their case loads makes any other kind of activity virtually impossible. While not disputing that caseworkers often have more clients than they can handle, this fact does not justify neglecting Phase II and III activities. Except in the most narrowly clinical of cases, the social work perspective almost inevitably raises the prospect of broader system change, and to reconcile oneself to a form of practice that does not even admit of the possibility is to reconcile oneself not to practising social work. Surely the problem of excessive caseloads is an issue that must be confronted in the light of what constitutes good social work practice.

A further objection to our approach concerns the likely resistance of agencies to their workers becoming involved in social action. Most casework agencies, particularly govern-ment agencies, are politically conservative and apt to view social action of any kind as disloyal, and even subversive. While it is true that practitioners who strive for policy change run the risk of censure by their employers, the practice model developed here does at least minimise the risk. After all, in the early stages of the campaign, all the worker is doing is bringing clients together for mutual support and discussion. A campaign of social action does not begin unless or until clients themselves are willing to work for change and prepared to take responsibility for leading the campaign. The worker need not, indeed should not, speak for them.

**A case example**

Steven is the 23-year-old, Australian-born son of Polish immigrants to Australia. He has an older sister who married a few years ago and followed her husband to another state and a better job. For his part, Steven mostly lives at home but he often moves away for weeks or months at a time. Sometimes he tells his parents where he is going, sometimes he does not. Steven's problems began in his last year of school; prior to that he had been a good student, having scored in the top 5 per cent of his class in his penultimate year. Steven had also been a popular boy, and although he preferred the company of his more rebellious peers, he himself was never in any kind of serious trouble.

Steven began his last year at school well enough. He saw plenty of his friends and, although he never set any world study endurance records, he was doing enough to be confident of a good pass and a place in economics at university if he wanted it. It was during final term that everything started to fall apart. To begin with all Steven's parents noticed was that he turned his record player up much louder than usual and locked himself in his room for long periods of time. Apart from his father's occasional cry of 'Turn that bloody thing down!', Steven's parents were remarkably tolerant of the deafening rock music sessions, putting his behaviour down to the stress of final year exams. As the weeks went by, though, Steven's behaviour began to change in more distressing ways. He would emerge from the private music sessions irascible and sullen. He stopped seeing his friends too, and study went entirely by the wayside. Probably because he was scared of his father, Steven seemed to save his worst for his mother. He would shout at her if she asked anything of him and sometimes he would burst out of his room and roar obscenities for no apparent reason. On one occasion he even struck his mother, but she did not dare tell Steven's father because he is a big and powerful man who has always settled disputes with Steven by literally thrashing him outside.

The incident that first brought Steven to hospital occurred about 3.00 a.m. one morning. People up and down the street were pounded out of their sleep by Steven's deafening music and, when his father vaulted out of bed to quell the din, what he saw stopped him in his tracks. Steven was squatting on his desk dressed only in underpants. His head had been shaved and he had scrawled his mother's lipstick around his mouth and eyes. Steven pressed his hands against his ears as he rocked his head from side to side. He was visibly frightened and he lunged at his father as any animal does when backed into a corner.

That was Steven's first psychotic episode and the beginning of what has been a seven-year, mostly involuntary, association with psychiatric hospitals, nurses, psychologists, psychiatrists, social workers, occupational therapists and others in the helping professions. After changing their minds a few times, psychiatrists nowadays seem settled on their diagnosis of schizophrenia. It transpired that Steven had been hearing an accusatory voice for many months before this incident. The voice would say the words, 'poofter' and 'kill or be killed', and Steven had to play his music as loudly as he could to shut the voice out.

That may have been Steven's first breakdown but it was not to be his last, and there is an unmistakable pattern to almost all his psychotic episodes. He normally starts by dressing in bright and ostentatious clothing and his behaviour becomes extremely garrulous. After a week or two he turns sullen, shaves his head and dons the hard, drab denim gear that befits his altered mood. Sometimes he is violent, always he is difficult and unpredictable, and always there is the one accusatory male voice saying, 'poofter', 'kill or be killed' or some other cryptic and threatening phrase. The hospital doctors who have treated Steven over the years arrest his psychosis in a chemical straitjacket and posit quite plausible theories about fear of homosexuality, over-involved parents and various developmental aberrations. Steven has been in counselling at one time or another with just about every profession represented in the hospital, and family therapy has been tried many times.

From a social work perspective these strategies are inadequate because they assume that the answer to Steven's problems lies only inside his head or the heads of him and his parents together. Steven does have a psychiatric disorder and psychotherapy and medication are probably worth including in a more comprehensive intervention plan but Steven's disorder is only part of a much wider problem comprised of many interconnecting factors, and an adequate response to his predicament must look beyond his head to the broader social and phenomenological world that he inhabits.

Consider the following additional details of Steven's life. Steven's parents are refugees from a Europe ravaged by the Second World War. His father is a lowly-paid council labourer who has put all his energies into educating his children and preparing them for a more secure life than he has enjoyed. Steven's mother has never been able to manage English so she spends most of her life inside the house doting on Steven and worrying about what people outside the house may be saying about or doing to her. In fact, both Steven's parents could be called suspicious people, a characteristic which is understandable given their wartime experiences. Because of the inwardness and vicarious ambition of his parents, Steven has always found home a pressurised place to be. This is a worrying aspect of Steven's social environment because emotional intensity is known to exacerbate schizophrenia. Because of his age and because of the atmosphere at home, it probably would be helpful for Steven to live elsewhere, but where can he go? He is unemployed and poor. His only income is unemployment benefit which not only is the lowest of all social security payments but even proscribes the niggardly fringe benefits provided to other social security beneficiaries. Steven applied for a pension once but was refused because the Commonwealth medical officer was understandably reluctant to label a perfectly healthy 23-year-old man an invalid. There are very few accommodation options for a man like Steven: about the only places he can afford are night shelters, hostels for psychiatric patients and the odd boarding house for alcoholics.

Due to his being unemployed, Steven is also unoccupied for much of the day. He sleeps for as long as he can and stays up until the early hours of the morning listening to hard rock and amusing himself with music magazines and fanciful dreams of life as a star. The social psychologist Jahoda (1979) has pointed out that without work there is no leisure and, more importantly, there is no order to the day and nothing to tie one to reality. Such circumstances promote disorientation and mental disorder. The most obvious solution would be for Steven to find work or some other activity to organise his life around but that has not been possible for him to achieve. Despite being 23, he has no qualifications or work experience. He is a likeable character but even on a good day somewhat eccentric, and he does not cope well with the stress of job interviews or having to perform in front of others. As a result, his job applications have always been unsuccessful and he has given up trying to find paid work altogether now. To make matters worse, neither the local Community Youth Support Scheme (CYSS) nor any of the State's sheltered workshops will take Steven; they have an unwritten policy of excluding psychiatric patients because of the trouble they cause. Being unemployed, Steven's friends tend to be marginalised and unemployed themselves and, to relieve the boredom, most of them drink too much and use marijuana when they can afford it. Steven naturally joins in but mind-altering drugs like alcohol and marijuana eventually precipitate a psychotic episode and for his own sake Steven really should drink less and avoid drugs altogether.

The whole unhappy situation is compounded by the hospital's lack of follow-up care. Until very recently, hospital policy was that, apart from infrequent outpatient visits to psychiatrists, responsibility for Steven's care ceased on discharge, at which time he became the responsibility of the so-called 'generic welfare services'. But, as we have already seen, this is not a policy that was ever negotiated with the community agencies themselves. For their part, community workers and parents are hostile towards psychiatric hospitals because they have enormous trouble getting hospitals to respond when patients become floridly psychotic.

In summary, Steven's is a *social* problem. On the one hand, he is only ever readmitted because his behaviour is intolerable to *others* and, on the other hand, his social situation is implicated in his recurring psychotic episodes.

The caseworker assigned to this case began with Steven himself. She tried to explore Steven's situation from his own perspective. She tried to look outwards from the hospital and concern herself with the issue of how Steven's social situation could be modified to make his life happier and more productive when he left hospital. The worker thought about engaging Steven in counselling around what she saw as latent sexual problems but, given the oversupply of psychotherapists in the hospital, she decided to leave that to others. At a level beyond Steven is his microsystem or the people and groups Steven has an ongoing relationship with: his parents, friends, and even professional staff such as social security personnel and hospital workers. In her analysis of the microsystem, the worker sought answers to three interrelated questions: (a) are these relationships somehow implicated in Steven's inability to survive in the community; (b) can these relationships be made more supportive in the future; (c) is there scope to foster additional supportive relationships outside the hospital?

The worker felt that she and Steven made some progress in these matters but even at this microsystem level the influence of broader policy issues was keenly felt. For example, it was difficult for Steven to build supportive relationships if he had no affordable option but to live at home with his parents, and the fact that to all intents and purposes recreational and vocational avenues were closed to him meant that he had little to build a life around. Nevertheless, Steven and his caseworker did the best they could, exploring ways of structuring the day, building in regular periods of activity outside the house and enlisting the support of Steven's only real friend (an old school mate) in occasionally taking him out and helping him to monitor and moderate his behaviour. This latter arrangement was welcomed by Steven, who recognised that early intervention was his best chance of avoiding involuntary detention in hospital. Under the assumption that a broader social network would reduce their over-involvement with Steven, the caseworker helped Steven's parents find a Polish club where difficulty with English would be no impediment to the formation of new friendships. At the level of the mesosystem, the caseworker tried to build a better working relationship between Steven's immediate social network and the hospital itself. With Steven's agreement, Steven and his parents undertook to keep in regular contact with his caseworker so that intervention could begin before the situation deteriorated to the point where hospitalisation was the only option. Steven agreed to visits from his caseworker provided that she did not tell his parents anything against his wishes. This simple step eventually resulted in the formation of a link between Steven's tenuous friendship network and the hospital, as his unemployed friends would occasionally call his caseworker when they recognised the signs of an imminent psychotic episode.

In Steven's case we also have seen the crucial importance of decisions taken by people he would never meet about such matters as housing for disadvantaged groups, the treatment of unemployment beneficiaries, admission criteria for CYSS programmes and sheltered workshops, and the outpatient services of psychiatric hospitals. It follows that a thorough-going solution to Steven's problems had to find ways of dealing with problems occurring at the exosystem level. These were not issues which Steven and his caseworker could influence in the short term; indeed, they were not issues that either fully understood. But both because she could see it leading to change at the level of the exosystem and because of the mutual support to be gained from it, Steven's caseworker began running small group meetings for schizophrenia sufferers and their families. At these meetings participants shared their problems and discussed practical solutions. In the early stages group members were constantly surprised by how much they had in common: over-reliance on parents, idleness and isolation, lack of vocational and recreational outlets, a chronic shortage of affordable accommodation for young psychiatric patients, the unresponsiveness of psychiatric hospitals, and so the list went on. As time went by the fifteen or so participants formed themselves into an association dedicated to promoting the interests of psychiatric patients and their families. A public meeting was planned; posters and leaflets were designed and distributed, and one or two of the more confident group members were interviewed on radio and television.

Approximately 500 people attended the public meeting at which a constitution was adopted and a committee elected. It was also decided that the association would produce a monthly newsletter and this has served ever since as the primary vehicle for keeping members in touch and mobilising support for the association's various projects. All but one of the committee members were drawn from the original family support group, but it was decided that committee meetings would be open to all association members anyway and, because meetings were run quite informally, there was always ample opportunity for any member of the association to express an opinion or place an issue on the agenda. The caseworker was elected as an ordinary member of the committee but her involvement decreased as time went by and she eventually resigned before her term of office expired.

The committee began with the relatively modest goal of establishing a half-way house for young psychiatric patients but their success in securing funding for this project soon spawned other projects and more far-reaching demands, such as an end to the discriminatory policies of generic welfare agencies, and calls for the decentralisation of resources away from hospitals and into community-based services run by boards on which patients and their families would hold the balance of power. The association became the accepted lobby group for psychiatric patients in that state, and branches have now been established throughout the country. Links were recently formed with the Unemployed Workers Union for the purpose of lobbying the federal government for more diverse vocational and recreational outlets for the unemployed as well as for greater spending on job creation programmes. The association's agenda of reform has become more sophisticated and more far-reaching over time and no government minister or civil servant can now afford to ignore its opinions.

**Social casework and the radical agenda**

This book opened with the radical objection to casework. It looked at the inadequacy of exclusively psychological approaches to human distress and it identified the potential of casework to blame the victims of structural injustice by looking inside their heads for a solution. The model outlined in these pages is intended to overcome this fundamental inadequacy of casework without rejecting casework itself. The book has been built on the conviction that casework, or to be more accurate *social* casework, is worth doing not only because of its immediate benefits to clients but because psychological change in the poor and marginalised is necessary if lasting structural change is to occur. Thus, the real debate between radical and conservative elements within social work ought not to be about *whether* to do casework, but *how*.

From a radical viewpoint the present approach could be said to suffer potentially serious, if not fatal, deficiencies. Underlying these deficiencies is the model's apparent acceptance of the fundamental assumptions of society without challenge. Up to now all our attention has been focused on minor social reform, and it is frequently said that reformism cannot be successful in solving fundamental social problems; indeed, that reformism is the antithesis of radical change. This objection to reformism is sometimes based on the notion that incrementalism is inconsistent with radical change. Truly 'radical' change, it is sometimes assumed, involves dramatic and far-reaching departures from existing arrangements, not the kind of minor concessions and policy changes discussed in the latter part of this book. But such a view is ignorant of history: with very few exceptions, all social change, including revolutionary change, has begun as a series of small departures. Revolution is more than the overthrow of those in power or the replacement of a particular system. It is a change in culture and psychology as much as in economics and politics, and for this reason revolutionary change will necessarily have incremental aspects. Radical workers may conceptualise and utilise incremental changes quite differently from the way conservative workers do. Nonetheless, the incremental nature of change efforts does not necessarily distinguish between radical and conservative social work practice. Similarly, reformism cannot be equated with changes that are non-militant or peaceful. As we saw in Chapter 5, Alinsky's (1969, 1971) community organising tactics could be militant to the point of violence, yet he has been denounced by radical activists for his liberal pluralist views.

A more sophisticated critique of social work practice looks to the *nature* of change, not just its size or its tactics. The most trenchant critics of reformism accuse it seeking change and improvement only within the boundaries of what is, of failing to challenge the superstructure or fundamental nature of society. Indeed, reformism can be closely linked with the political forms of liberal pluralism which sees public policy as emerging from the interplay of sectional interests and the agreements worked out among sub-groups of the population. The role of government is to act as a kind of referee between competing and antagonistic groups. Faith in the beneficial effects of competition and the negotiated settlements of interest groups is a fundamental part of the ideology of reformism. Reformism, like liberal pluralism, is not a critical ideology.

It is true that the major weakness of reformism is that it tends to isolate change efforts from one another and it does not always recognise the linkages between specific change efforts and changes in the whole. As long as the analysis and struggle are at the level of seeking resources for a particular group or a particular area of need, gains made by reformist groups can (and often do) result in a loss of resources to other equally exploited groups and in the failure to consider dilemmas common to *all* marginalised individuals. The latent effect of this kind of struggle is to promote conflict between the disadvantaged in society. Reformists do not often see that social problems are rooted in social structures, and by focusing on the specific needs of a specific client group reformists can see only the symptoms of problems, not the problems themselves.

From the caseworker's standpoint this kind of analysis can have the effect of paralysing rather than radicalising practice. There is clearly little point in working for the sectional interests of one's clients if the concessions gained are going to work against, rather than for, social justice. Having come to this sometimes painful realisation about reformism, potential activists frequently become disheartened about their practice and daunted by the magnitude of the 'real' problem confronting them, forcing many of them to take refuge in empty symbolic actions and rhetoric. But what this kind of reaction overlooks is that the involvement by marginalised groups in pressing their own sectional interests is a vital, even essential, stage in the radicalisation of the poor. The age-old casework injunction to 'start where the client is' is as true of social action as it is of psychotherapy. Immersed as they are in a daily struggle for survival, most public welfare clients can see no further than their own immediate needs. It is pointless, if not insulting, to exhort such people to struggle for long-term structural change. The political conservatism of the poor is well known, and at least some of their reluctance to engage in radical social action can be attributed to their inability to see how the struggle helps *them*. What will help them now is reform. Caseworkers know that complex psychological change is best achieved by a series of successive approximations to the desired result and, viewed in this light, engagement in minor reformist activity would be a logical stage in the behavioural hierarchy.

For marginalised and isolated casework clients, involvement in communal reformist activity creates the conditions for at least four major advances in their political education. Taken together, these achievements provide a rationale and justification for the model outlined at the beginning of this book. First, involvement in reformist activity is likely to provide clients with an experience of wresting tangible concessions from policy-makers through persistence and assertiveness. In other words, previously powerless individuals begin to see that social action can produce results. As discussed in Chapter 3, a major obstacle to social action on the part of the poor is their expectation that responding will not work. This 'learned helplessness' is only overcome through exposure to subjectively important, controllable life events; and minor concessions, such as the improvement of local child-care facilities, can be both subjectively important to women in the area and potentially achievable in the short-term. Provided the struggle is successful, it will help to erode the psychology of powerlessness that keeps the poor submerged.

A second benefit to be gained from involvement in reformist campaigns is the experience of communal action. Fundamental to the radical agenda is a sense of class consciousness on the part of the poor, and this kind of awareness is unlikely to develop unless the conditions are created in which marginalised individuals are able to see that their seemingly private problems are in fact shared by others. In the author's own practice experience, the realisation that others share precisely the same difficulties as they do is an intensely liberating experience for most clients. It is an experience which enables marginalised individuals to experience their connectedness to other marginalised individuals.

A third important, if frustrating, benefit of reformist activity is that clients frequently come to see their victories for what they are: perfunctory and tokenistic. While some clients can be expected to terminate their involvement with the group after certain immediate demands have been met, others will see that such things as a new child-care centre or alterations to a tenancy agreement with public housing authorities do not fundamentally alter their situation. These individuals are likely to remain politically active, increasing both the range and depth of their demands. The political agenda of the 'competent' people in Kieffer's (1987) study (see Chapter 6) eventually expanded well beyond the problem that first motivated them to act. As they participated in the political process, they saw the need for more fundamental change than they first thought necessary. Both their vision and their sense of what was possible expanded. A final, and related, benefit of engagement in reformist campaigns is that participants learn first-hand about the political process and this is essential knowledge whatever one's political agenda.

The best hope for radical change in the Western world rests with what Galper (1975, 1980) has referred to as 'the bottom up/collective approach', by which he means building on the commitment of small collectives, at work on a variety of different projects in a variety of locations (see also Oglesby and Shaull, 1967). In this book we have explored the potential for such groups to emerge from casework. By working to establish democratic collectives of clients united by a common social problem, caseworkers set the stage for more radical change in the future. The struggle for radical change will become a reality when these small, locally organised collectives come to see and unite around the larger issues which transcend their individual campaigns. From this viewpoint, then, the case illustration described above entered a most important stage when the patients and their families and friends decided to join forces with other the Unemployed Workers Union to lobby for increased recreational and vocational opportunities for the unemployed. This is an ideal arrangement, for it succeeds in integrating larger social issues with the daily problems that affect each marginalised group separately.

Ultimately, however, whether or not casework promotes or impedes radical social change will be determined at the assessment stage of our model. In Chapter 2 it was pointed out that it is because of deficiencies at the assessment stage that traditional approaches to casework have been so inadequate. As Baran (1969) suggested, over twenty years ago, the usual notion of person-in-situation adopted by caseworkers refers to little more than the effect of the most immediate environment on the person. He referred to the casework viewpoint as 'socio-psychologism', for although it recognises that individuals cannot be understood in isolation, it stops far short of a truly social analysis. As Baran put it:

> The character of man [sic] is the product of the social order in which he is born, in which he grows up, and the air of which he inhales throughout his life; it is its result and indeed one of its most significant aspects. Yet it is of the utmost importance to understand that what is meant by 'social order' in Marxian theory is at most only a distant cousin of the notion of 'society' as employed in socio-psychologism. The latter, it will be recalled, refers to 'environment' to 'interpersonal relations', and to similar aspects of what constitutes the surface of social existence. The former, on the other hand, encompasses the attained stage of the development of productive forces, the mode and relations of production, the form of social domination prevailing at any given time, all together constituting the basic structure of the existing social organization. (p. 98)

Thus the social work tradition of seeing people within a 'social context' is a perspective which allows for significant differences of interpretation and, in the end, the worker's interpretation of what constitutes the 'social context' is a profoundly political decision. If the life situation of each client is not understood in terms of the fundamental nature of society as whole, then the social assessment will go up to and not beyond the client and his or her immediate environment. It is true that caseworkers have a history of failing to move from a consideration of some specifics of psychology and the social situation to a perspective on the totality of the human condition. Social casework has tended to operate on the basis of a limited social-psychological view that does not look sufficiently deeply into the social roots of people's dilemmas. Consequently, it has not developed strategies to deal with the more profound causal factors behind these dilemmas. It is hoped that the present model may allow caseworkers to develop such strategies in the context of their daily activities.

In summary, then, casework is not *inherently* conservative as its detractors so frequently argue; it is only so because of the way it is commonly defined and practised. Moreover psychological liberation must occur for political struggle to be engaged in. As Galper (1975) put it in his classic work, 'The idea of individuals struggling to maximize themselves as people, to make the most of their potential as human beings in and through a changed society, has radical psychological and political implications if freed of its specific current historical political trappings' (p. 136). Rather than be seen as exclusively psychotherapeutic or as directed to social adjustment, casework as represented here is focused on the development of political awareness and on the willingness to struggle for change.

# References

Abramson, L. Y., Seligman, M. E. P. and Teasdale, J. D. (1978) 'Learned helplessness in humans: critique and reformulation', *Journal of Abnormal Psychology*, 87, 49–74.

Alinsky, S. (1969) *Reveille for Radicals*, New York, Vintage Books.

Alinsky, S. (1971) *Rules for Radicals*, New York, Random House.

Anderson, J. (1981) *Social Work Methods and Processes*, Belmont, Wadsworth.

Ashcroft, B. and Jackson, K. (1974) 'Adult education and social action', in D. Jones and M. Mayo (eds) *Community Work One*, London, Routledge & Kegan Paul.

Austin, L. N. (1948) 'Trends in differential treatment in social casework', *Journal of Social Casework*, 29, 203–11.

Bailey, R. and Brake, M. (eds) 1977 *Radical Social Work*, London, Edward Arnold

Baird, J. (1985) *Budgets for Community Groups*, Melbourne, Victorian Council of Social Service.

Baldock, P. (1974) *Community Work and Social Work*, London, Routledge & Kegan Paul.

Bandura, A. (1977) *Social Learning Theory*, Englewood-Cliffs, NJ, Prentice-Hall.

Baran, P. A. (1969) *The Longer View*, New York, Monthly Review Press.

Barber, J. G. (1982) 'Unemployment and helplessness', *Australian Social Work*, 35, 3–10.

Barber, J. G. (1985) 'Mental health policy in South Australia – a job half done', *Australian Journal of Social Issues*, 20, 75–86.

Bartlett, H. M. (1970) *The Common Base of Social Work Practice*, Washington, DC, National Association of Social Workers.

Batten, T. R. (1965a) *Communities and Their Development*, Chicago, University of Chicago Press.

Batten, T. R. (1965b) *The Human Factor in Community Work*, London, Oxford University Press.

Batten, T. R. and Batten, M. (1967) *The Non-Directive Approach in Group and Community Work*, London, Oxford University Press.

Beck, A. T. (1967) *Depression: Clinical, Experimental and Theoretical Aspects*, New York, Harper & Row.

Beck, A. T., Rush, A. J., Shaw, B. F. and Emery, G. (1979) *Cognitive Therapy for Depression*, New York, Guilford.

Bedics, B. C. and Doelker, R. (1983) 'Mobilizing informal resources for rural communities', *Human Services in the Rural Environment*, 8, 18–23.

Belsky, J. (1980) 'Child maltreatment. An ecological approach', *American Psychologist*, 35, 320–35.

Biddle, W. W. and Biddle, L. J. (1965) *The Community Development Process: The Rediscovery of Local Initiative*, New York, Holt, Rinehart & Winston.

Boehm, W. (1958) 'The nature of social work', *Social Work*, 3, 10–19.

Brager, G. and Specht, H. (1973) *Community Organizing*, New York, Columbia University Press.

Brehm, J. W. (1972) *Responses to Loss of Freedom: A Theory of Psychological Reactance*, Morristown, N. J., General Learning Press.

Brieland, D. (1987) 'History and evolution of social work practice', *Encyclopedia of Social Work,* (18th edn), Washington, DC, National Association of Social Workers.

Bronfenbrenner, U. (1979) *The Ecology of Human Development: Experiments by Nature and Design*, Cambridge, Mass, Harvard University Press.

Caplan, N. and Nelson, S. D. (1973) 'On being useful. The nature and consequnces of psychological research on social problems', *American Psychologist*, 28, 199–211.

Carkhuff, R. R. (1969a) *Helping and Human Relations. Vol. 1: Selection and Training*, New York, Holt, Rinehart & Winston.

Carkhuff, R. R. (1969b) *Helping and Human Relations. Vol. 2: Practice and Research*, New York, Holt, Rinehart & Winston.

Carkhuff, R. R. and Anthony, W. A. (1979) *The Skills of Helping: An Introduction to Counseling*, Amherst, MA, Human Resource Development Press.

Carkhuff, R. R. and Berensen, B. G. (1976) *Teaching as Treatment*, Amherst, MA, Human Resource Development Press.

Clancy, P. (1981) *How to Chair a Meeting*, Sydney, Trade Union Information and Research Centre.

Cohen, P. (1989) 'Hard bargains to be struck on funding', *Social Work Today*, (20 July), 8–9.

Cohen, P. and Eaton, L. (1989) 'Councils given key role but funding doubts remain', *Social Work Today*, (20 July), 2–3.

Community Action (1975) 'How to organise and run public meetings', *Community Action*, 19.

Community Liaison (1978) 'Managing voluntary organisations', *Community Liaison*, 1, 95–104.

Compton, B. and Galaway, B. (1984) *Social Work Processes*, Homewood, IL, Dorsey Press.

Delbecq, A. L. and Van de Ven, A. H. (1977) 'A group process model for problem identification and program planning', in N. Gilbert and H. Specht (eds), *Planning For Welfare*, Englewood Cliffs, NJ, Prentice-Hall.

Dunham, A. (1959) 'What is the job of the community organization worker?' in E. B. Harper and A. Dunham (eds), *Community Organization in Action*, New York, Association Press.

Dunham, A. (1963) 'Some principles of community development', *International Review of Community Development*, 11, 141–51.

Dunham, A. (1970) *The New Community Organization*, New York, Thomas Crowell.

D'Zurilla, T. J. and Goldfried, M. R. (1971) 'Problem solving and behavior modification', *Journal of Abnormal Psychology*, 78, 107–26.

Egan, G. (1985) *The Skilled Helper*, Monterey, CA, Brooks/Cole.

Epstein, L. (1980) *Helping People: The Task-Centred Approach*, St Loius, MO, C. V. Mosby.

Fawcett, B. (1989) 'Community care – the answer to Griffiths at last', *Social Work Today*, (20 July), 26.

Feather, N. T. and Barber, J. G. (1983) 'Unemployment and depressive reactions', *Journal of Abnormal Psychology*, 92, 185–95.

Fisher, J. (1984) *Let the People Decide: Neighbourhood Organizing in America*, Boston, Twayne.

Fisher, R. (1987) 'Community organizing in historical perspective: a typology', in F. M. Cox, J. L. Erlich, J. Rothman and J. E. Tropman (eds), *Strategies of Community Organization* (4th edn), Itasca, IL, Peacock.

Fosterling, F. (1985) 'Attributional retraining: a review', *Psychological Bulletin*, 98, 495–512.

Freire (1970) 'Cultural action and conscientization', *Harvard Educational Review*, 40, 459.

Freire, P. (1972a) *Cultural Action for Freedom*, Harmondsworth, Penguin.

Freire, P. (1972b) *Pedagogy of the Oppressed*, Harmondsworth, Penguin.

Galper, J. H. (1975) *The Politics of Social Service*, Englewood Cliffs, NJ, Prentice-Hall.

Galper, J. H. (1980) *Social Work: A Radical Perspective*, Englewood Cliffs, NJ, Prentice-Hall.

Germain, C. B. and Gitterman, A. (1980) *The Life Model of Social Work Practice*, New York, Columbia University Press.

Germain, C. B. and Hartman, A. (1980) 'People and ideas in the history of social work', *Social Casework*, 61, 323–31.

Gilbert, N. and Specht, H. (1977) 'Process versus task in social planning', *Social Work*, 22, 178–83.

Goldstein, H. (1973) *Social Work Practice: A Unitary Approach*, Columbia, University of South Carolina Press.

Gordon, W. E. (1965) 'Toward a social work frame of reference', *Journal of Education for Social Work*, 1, 19–26.

Gordon, W. (1969) 'Basic constructs for an integrative and generative conception of social work', in G. Hearn (ed.), *The General Systems Approach: Contributions Toward an Holistic Conception of Social Work*, New York, Council on Social Work Education.

Griffiths, R. (1988) *Community Care: Agenda for Action*, London, HMSO.

Grosser, C. F. (1973) *New Directions in Community Organization*, New York, Praeger.

Grosser, C. F. and Mondros, J. (1985) 'Pluralism and participation: the political action approach, in S. H. Taylor and Roberts 1985.

Gulbenkian Foundation Study Group (1968) *Community Work and Social Change*, London, Routledge & Kegan Paul.

Haggstrom, W. C. (1987) 'The tactics of organization building', in F. M. Cox, J. L. Erlich, J. Rothman and J. E. Tropman (eds), *Strategies of Community Organization* (4th edn), Itasca, IL, Peacock.

Halliday, H. (1980) *Community Organisation Guide. A Manual on How to Administer and Organise Community Groups*, Melbourne, Victorian Council of Social Service.

Hamilton, G. (1937) 'Basic concepts on social casework', *Family*, 18, 147–59.

Hamilton, G. (1941) 'The underlying philosophy of social casework', *Family*, 23, 139–48.

Hamilton, G. (1951) *Theory and Practice of Social Casework*, New York, Columbia University Press.

Hartman, A. (1970) 'To think about the unthinkable', *Social Casework*, 51, 467–74.

Heider, F. (1958) *The Psychology of Interpersonal Relations*, New York, Wiley.

Henderson, P. and Thomas, D. N. (1980) *Skills in Neighbourhood Work*, London, George Allen & Unwin.

Heptinstall, D. (1989) 'At the end of the journey', *Social Work Today*, (27 July), 16–17.

Hepworth, D. H. and Larsen, J. (1986) *Direct Social Work Practice: Theory and Skills*, Chicago, IL, Dorsey Press.

Hiroto, D. S. and Seligman, M. E. P. (1975) 'Generality of learned helplessness in man', *Journal of Personality and Social Psychology*, 31, 311–27.

Hollis, E. V. and Taylor, A. L. (1951) *Social Work Education in the United States*, New York, Columbia University Press.

Hollis, F. (1964) *Social Casework: A Psychosocial Therapy*, New York, Random House.

Hollis, F. (1968) *A Typology of Casework Treatment*, New York, Family Service Association of America.

Hollis, F. (1970) 'The psychosocial approach to the practice of casework', in R. W. Roberts and R. H. Nee (eds), *Theories of Social Casework*, Chicago, University of Chicago Press.

Hollis, F. (1977) 'Social casework: the psychosocial approach', in *Encyclopedia of Social Work* (17th edn), Washington DC, National Association of Social Workers, 1300–07.

Hudson, B. L. and Macdonald,, G. M. (1986) *Behavioural Social Work: An Introduction*, Lara, Macmillan

Hunter, M. (1984) *Marketing Handbook*, Adelaide, South Australia, South Australian Council of Social Service.

Ivey, A. E. (1983) *Intentional Interviewing and Counseling*, Monterly, CA, Brooks/Cole.

Jahoda, M. (1979) 'The impact of unemployment in the 1930s and 1970s', *Bulletin of The British Psychological Society*, 32, 309–14.

Janchill, M. P. (1969) 'Systems concepts in casework theory and practice', *Social Casework*, 50, 74–82.

Janis, I. L. and Mann, L. (1977) *Decision Making*, New York, The Free Press.

Jones, M. A. (1977) *Organisation and Social Planning in Australian Local Government*, Melbourne, Heinemann.

Kahn, S. (1970) *How People Get Power. Organizing Oppressed Communities for Action*, New York, McGraw-Hill.

Kahn, S. (1982) *Organizing*, New York, McGraw-Hill.

Keith-Lucas, A. (1972) *The Giving and Taking of Help*, Chapel Hill, University of North Carolina Press.

Khinduka, S. K. (1987) 'Community development: potentials and limitations', in F. M. Cox, J. L. Erlich, J. Rothman and J. E. Tropman (eds), *Strategies of Community Organization* (4th ed), Itasca, IL, Peacock.

Kish, L. (1965) *Survey Sampling*, New York, Wiley.

Kieffer, C. H. (1984) 'Citizen empowerment: a developmental perspective', *Prevention in Human Services*, 4, 9–36.

Kotler, P. (1975) *Marketing for Non-Profit Organisations*, Englewood Cliffs, NJ, Prentice Hall.

Kramer, R. M. and Specht, H. (eds) (1983) *Readings in Community Organization Practice*, Englewood Cliffs, NJ, Prentice Hall.

Lappin, B. (1985) 'Community development: beginnings in social work enabling', in S. H. Taylor and Roberts (1985).

Lathey, R. G. (1974) *Chairman, Secretary and Discussion Leader*, Melbourne, Rigby.

Layden, M. A. (1982) 'Attributional style therapy', in C. Antaki and C. Brewin (eds), *Attributions and Psychological Change*, London, Academic Press.

Leigh, A. (1989) 'Last chance to get the plans right', *Social Work Today*, (18 Jan), 20–21.

Lerner, M. P. (1979) 'Surplus powerlessness', *Social Policy*, (Jan./Feb.), 19–27.

Lindzey, G. and Aronson, E. (eds) (1968) *The Handbook of Social Psychology, Vol. 2: Research Methods*, Reading, MA, Addison-Wesley.

Maier, S. F., Seligman, M. E. P. and Solomon, R. L. (1969) 'Pavlovian fear conditioning and learned helplessness: effects on escape and avoidance behavior of (a) the CS–US contingency and (b) the independence of the US voluntary responding', in B. A. Campbell and R. M. Church (eds), *Punishment and Aversive Behavior*, New York, Appleton-Century-Crofts.

Mayer, J. E. and Timms, N. (1970) *The Client Speaks: Working-Class Impressions of Casework*, London, Routledge & Kega-Paul.

Meichenbaum, D. (1978) *Cognitive Behaviour Modification: An Integrative Approach*, New York, Plenum Press.

Meyer, C. H. (1983) *Clinical Social Work in an Ecological Systems Perspective*, New York, Columbia University Press.

Meyer, C. H. (1987) 'Direct practice in social work: an overview', *Encyclopedia of Social Work*, (18th ed), 409–22.

Middleman, R. and Goldberg, G. (1974) *Social Service Delivery: A Structural Approach to Social Work Practice*, New York, Columbia University Press.

Miller, I. W. and Norman, W. H. (1979) 'Learned helplessness in humans: a review and an attributional theory model', *Psychological Bulletin*, 86, 93–118.

Mills, C. Wright (1943) 'The professional ideology of social pathologists', *American Journal of Sociology*, 49, 165–80.

Morris, R. and Binstock, R. H. (1966) *Feasibility Planning for Social Change*, New York, Columbia University Press.

Moser, C. A. and Kalton, G. (1981) *Survey Methods in Social Investigation*, London, Heinnemann Educational Books.

Murphy, G. E. Simons, A. D., Wetzel, R. D. and Lustmann, P. J. (1984) 'Cognitive therapy and pharmacology singly and together in the treatment of depression', *Archives of General Psychiatry*, 41, 33–41.

Nelsen, J. C. (1980) *Communication Theory and Social Work Practice*, Chicago, University of Chicago Press.

Newstetter, W. I. (1947) 'The social intergroup process', *Proceedings of the National Conference of Social Work, 1947*, New York, Columbia University Press.

Norton, M. (1977) *Community Change. Directory of Social Change*, London. Wildwood House.

Oglesby, C. and Shaull, R. (1967) *Containment and Change*, New York, Macmillan.

Osborn, A. F. (1963) *Principles and Procedures of Creative Problem-Solving*, New York, Scribner's.

Overmier, J. B. and Seligman, M. E. P. (1967) 'Effects of inescapable shock upon subsequent escape and avoidance responding', *Journal of Comparative and Physiological Psychology*, 63, 28–33.

Panzer, B. (1983) 'Crisis intervention', in Meyer (1983).

Parad, H. (ed.) (1965) *Crisis Intervention*, New York, Columbia University Press.

Perlman, H. H. (1957) *Casework: A Problem-Solving Process*, Chicago, University of Chicago Press.

Perlman, H. H. (1968) *Persona: Social Role and Personality*, Chicago, University of Chicago Press.

Perlman, H. H. (1971) *Perspectives in Casework*, Philadelphia, Temple University Press.

Peterson, C. and Seligman, M. E. P. (1984) 'Causal explanations as a risk factor for depression: theory and evidence', *Psychological Review*, 91, 347–74.

Pincus, A. and Minahan, A. (1973) *Social Work Practice: Method and Model*, Itasca, IL, Peacock.

Piven, F. and Cloward, R. (1977) *Poor People's Movements: How They Succeed, Why They Fail*, New York, Pantheon.

Plant, R. (1974) *Community and Ideology*, London, Routledge & Kegan Paul.

Pumphrey, R. E. and Pumphrey, M. W. (1961) *The Heritage of American Social Work*. Itasca, IL, Peacock.

Rapoport, L. (1962) 'The state of crisis: some theoretical considerations', *Social Service Review*, 36, 211–17.

Rapoport, L. (1970) 'Crisis intervention as a mode of brief treatment', in R. Roberts and R. Nee (eds), *Theories of Social Casework*, Chicago, University of Chicago Press.

Reid, W. J. and Epstein, L. (1972) *Task-Centred Practice*, New York, Columbia University Press.

Reid, W. J. and Shyne, Q. W. (1969) *Brief and Extended Casework*, New York, Columbia University Press.

Reynolds, B. C. (1951) *Social Work and Social Living*, New York, Citadel.

Richmond, M. E. (1917) *Social Diagnosis*, New York, Russell Sage Foundation.

Richmond, M. E. (1922) *What is Social Casework? An Introductory Description*, New York, Russell Sage Foundation.

Ripple, L. (1964) *Motivation, Capacity, and Opportunity: Studies in Casework Theory and Practice*, Social Service Monographs, Chicago, University of Chicago Press.

Robinson, V. (1930) *A Changing Psychology in Social Case Work*, Chapel Hill, University of North Carolina Press.

Rogers, C. R. (1951) *Client-Centred Therapy*, Boston, Houghton-Mifflin.

Rogers, C. R. (1957) 'The necessary and sufficient conditions of therapeutic personality change', *Journal of Consulting Psychology*, 21, 95–103.

Rogers, C. R. (1961) *On Becoming a Person*, Boston, Houghton-Mifflin.

Rogers, C. R. (ed.) (1967) *The Therapeutic Relationship and its Impact*, Madison, WI, University of Wisconsin Press.

Rogers, C. R. (1975) 'Empathy, an unappreciated way of being', *Counselling Psychologist*, 21, 95–103.

Rooney, R. H. (1988) 'Socialization strategies for involuntary clients', *Social Casework*, (March), 130–40.

Ross, M. G. (1955) *Community Organization: Theory and Principles*, New York, Harper.

Ross, M. G. (1958) *Case Histories in Community Organization*, New York, Harper.

Ross, M. G. and Lappin, B. W. (1967) *Community Organization: Theory, Principles and Practice*, New York, Harper & Row.

Roth, S. (1980) 'A revised model of learned helplessness in humans', *Journal of Personality*, 48, 103–33.

Rothman, J. (1979) 'Three models of community organization practice', in F. M. Cox, J. L. Erlich, J. Rothman and J. E. Tropman (eds), *Strategies of Community Organization* (3rd ed), Itasca, IL, Peacock.

Rothman, J. and Tropman, J. E. (1987) 'Models of community organization and macro practice perspectives: their mixing and phasing', in F. M. Cox, J. L. Erlich, J. Rothman and J. E.

Tropman (eds), *Strategies of Community Organization* (4th edn), Itasca, IL, Peacock.

Ryan, W. (1971) *Blaming the Victim*, New York, Pantheon.

Schwartz, E. E. (1977) 'Macro social work: a practice in search of some theory', *Social Service Review*, 51, 201–27.

Scott, D. (1981) *Don't Mourn For Me . . . . Organise*, Sydney, Allen & Unwin.

Seligman, M. E. P. (1972) 'Learned helplessness', *Annual Review of Medicine*, 23, 407–12.

Seligman, M. E. P. (1975) *Helplessness. On Depression, Development and Death*, San Francisco, Freeman.

Seligman, M. E. P. (1978) 'Comment and integration', *Journal of Abnormal Psychology*, 87, 165–79.

Seligman, M. E. P., Maier, S. F. and Geer, J. H. (1968) 'Alleviation of learned helplessness in the dog', *Journal of Abnormal Psychology*, 73, 256–62.

Seligman, M. E. P., Maier, S. F. and Solomon, R. L. (1971) 'Unpredictable and uncontrollable aversive events', in F. R. Brush (ed), *Aversive Conditioning and Learning*, New York, Academic Press.

Siegel, L. M., Attkison, C. C., and Carson, L. G. (1978) 'Need identification and program planning in the community context', in C. C. Attkisson, W. A. Hargreaves, M. J. Horowitz and J. E. Sorensen (eds), *Evaluation of Human Service Programs*, New York, Academic Press. 215–49.

Simpkin, M. (1983) *Trapped With Welfare*, London, Macmillan.

Siporin, M. (1975) *Introduction to Social Work Practice*, New York, Macmillan.

Skinner, B. F. (1971) *Beyond Freedom and Dignity*, New York, Knopf.

Smalley, R. E. (1967) *Theory for Social Work Practice*, New York, Columbia University Press.

Smalley, R. E. (1977) 'Social casework: the functional approach', *Encyclopedia of Social Work* (17th edn), Washington, DC, National Association of Social Workers, 1195–206.

Stein, I. D. (1974) *Systems theory, science and social work*, Metuchen, NJ, Scarecrow.

Strean, H. (1971) *Social casework: theories in action*, Metuchen, NJ, Scarecrow.

Taft, J. (1937) 'The relation of function to process in social case work', *Journal of Social Work Processes*, 1, 1–18.

Taylor, H. M. and Mears, A. G. (1976) *The Right Way to Conduct Meetings, Conferences and Discussions*, Sydney, Kingswood Paperfronts.

Taylor, J. (1984) *The Grants Book*, Adelaide, South Australian Council of Social Service.

Taylor, S. H. and Roberts, R. W. (eds) (1985) *Theory and Practice of Community Social Work*, Englewood Cliffs, NJ, Prentice Hall.

Teasdale, J. D. (1985) 'Psychological treatments for depression: how do they work?', *Behaviour Research and Therapy*, 23, 157–65.

Teisiger, K. S. (1983) 'Evaluation of education for generalist practice', *Journal of Education for Social Work*, 19, 79–85.

Thomas, E. J. (ed.) (1967) *The Socio-behavioral Approach and Applications to Social Work*, New York, Council on Social Work Education.

Thomas, E. J. (1968) 'Selected sociobehavioural techniques and principles: an approach to interpersonal helping', *Social Work*, 13, 12–26.

Thomas, E. J. (1970) 'Behavioral modification and casework', in R. W. Roberts and R. H. Nee (eds), *Theories of Social Casework*, Chicago, University of Chicago Press, 183–218.

Turner, F. J. (ed.) (1983) *Differential Diagnosis and Treatment in Social Work*, New York, Free Press.

Turner, F. J. (1987) 'Psychosocial approach', in *Encyclopedia of Social Work* (18th edn), Washington, DC, National Association of Social Workers, 397–405.

Twelvetrees, A. (1982) *Community Work*, London, Macmillan

Vickery, A. (1974) 'A systems approach to social work intervention: its uses for work with individuals and families', *British Journal of Social Work*, 4, 389–403.

Victorian Council of Social Service (1981) *Reaching Decision Makers*, Melbourne, Victorian Council of Social Service.

Victorian Council of Social Service (1985) *Community Funding and Resource Guide*, Melbourne, Victorian Council of Social Service.

Wortman, C. B. and Brehn, J. W. (1975) 'Responses to uncontrollable outcomes: an integration of reactance theory and the learned helplessness model', in L. Berkowitz (ed.), *Advances in Experimental Social Psychology*, vol. 8, New York; Academic Press.

York, A.S. (1984) 'Towards a conceptual model of community social work', *British Journal of Social Work*, 14, 241–55.

# Index